TORQ
MOTTO W

CW01669520

Editor: Virginia Brisco

Text by Virginia Brisco, Shirley Everett, Bill Brisco

Photographs by Brian Everett

Layout and Design by Keith Poole

Published by
Torquay Pottery Collectors' Society, Torre Abbey, Torquay, Devon, England

In the name of God the
passionate the merciful,
seek refuge with the
malice of the lurking
the Genii and

This book is dedicated to the many men and women who toiled in the South Devon potteries, often for low wages, to produce the beautiful pots that we treasure today.

"When this you see remember me"

ACKNOWLEDGEMENTS

The majority of pots illustrated in the photographs are from the collections owned by the production team. However, we should also like to thank Mr and Mrs D. Barber, Mr and Mrs R. Wood, Miss M. Broderick and Mr J. Cook for the loan of additional pots from their collections for some of the photographs. Also the many members of the Torquay Pottery Collectors' Society who sent us mottoes for inclusion in the book. We are grateful to Mr F. K. Dart for permission to use the photographs of his father, Fred Dart, and grandfather, John Dart; also to Mrs Doris Brooker, daughter of Charlie Wonnacott, for a copy of the photograph of the Watcombe Pottery in fig. 52.

Fig. 1 (frontispiece). Aller Vale pot decorated with the Persian pattern and motto filled in with blue c.1890. Height 10" (25·4cm).

PREFACE

DURING the past ten years or so there has been an upsurge of interest in 'Torquay Pottery', the generic term for a wide variety of wares produced by more than a dozen potteries in the South Devon area over the last 120 years. Of all the styles produced, mottowares are probably the most widely known and to many people cottage wares are synonymous with 'Torquay Pottery'. The growing interest in this area of collecting has been reflected in the rapid increase in membership of the Torquay Pottery Collectors' Society and the desire for more information about the pottery. Most collectors are introduced to Torquay pottery through mottowares and this booklet is intended to provide a broad history of the subject and a comprehensive survey of the types of items that were made. Although the authors have researched the subject thoroughly and spoken to many old potters and fellow collectors through the T.P.C.S., this booklet does not claim to be the definitive authority and we welcome contributions and corrections where appropriate.

There are many other styles of Torquay pottery apart from mottowares and information about these will be published in future booklets. Meanwhile, we hope that collectors will join the T.P.C.S. and share their love of the pottery with like minded enthusiasts.

MOTTOWARES — A POTTED HISTORY

THE term "Mottoware" is used to describe any type of ceramics that has writing on it. This type of ware has a long history in Britain stretching back 2,000 years to the Roman empire. Some pots dating from this period have been seen with slip decoration and inscriptions. After the Roman occupation ended, decorative pottery seems to have gone into a decline, although functional items would have been made for use. By the sixteenth century pots with sayings were becoming popular again, some with mottoes such as "Amend they life and sin no more", others made to commemorate a special event such as a family wedding or christening or a Royal state event. Of these sixteenth century potters, Thomas Toft is probably the most well known and his mottowares were done in slip trailed over a clay body. Slip is a thin clay and water mixture which is applied by a technique similar to piping a cake. In other cases mottoes were scratched through a slip body (known as sgraffito) or painted on.

During the seventeenth and eighteenth centuries most country potteries would have made slip decorated mottowares for the local market. With the growth of larger potteries during the Industrial Revolution new techniques such as transfer printing, were developed for mottowares, e.g. Sunderland pottery. The Industrial Revolution led to the decline of many country potteries because the larger Staffordshire potteries could mass produce more cheaply; also to the rapidly expanding working classes the thin slip cast wares were more dainty and emulated the fine porcelain favoured by the well-to-do. However, in some areas notably North Devon, the tradition of hand made pottery with its quaint rustic mottoes continued throughout the nineteenth century.

North Devon had a long history of potting, partly based on good supplies of local clay but also on clay imported through towns such as Bideford,

Fig. 2. Stein shaped jug, 9" tall (23cm), showing sgraffito lettering scratched through cream slip to expose darker clay beneath. Made by Aller Vale c.1895. The motto is a quotation from Burns.

maintaining the tradition of slip and sgraffito decoration. However, in 1869 a new band of clay was discovered at Watcombe, near Torquay and this was to spawn a batch of new potteries in South Devon, so much so that by the early twentieth century their output had overtaken that of their North Devon counterparts.

The Watcombe Terracotta Clay Company was established in 1869 to exploit the new resource, and some five years later its rival, The Torquay Terracotta Company began production at nearby Hele Cross, Torquay, to use other recently discovered clay seams, some of which came from the local cemetery conveniently situated across the road! Both these companies, though, spurned traditional country styles in favour of elegant classical urns, vases, statuettes, etc. (which were still fashionable), and so they recruited their labour force from Staffordshire. It was therefore not until the 1880s that slip and sgraffito mottowares came to South Devon through the philanthropic motives of Mr.

John Phillips, owner of the Aller Vale pottery at Kingskerswell, near Newton Abbot. A clay works had existed there for some years manufacturing domestic terracotta (chimneys, flower pots, etc.) and Mr. Phillips acquired it in 1871. John Phillips was a firm supporter of the ideals of William Morris and had encouraged the establishment of local cottage Art Schools to train young people in traditional arts and crafts. In 1881, following a fire at the Aller works, Mr. Phillips decided to reopen it as an Art Pottery and what more natural than that they should concentrate on slipware.

The early "Torquay" mottowares

The earliest mottowares made at the Aller Vale Art Pottery were very heavily potted and have a rustic individuality. The slip decoration was often of a stylised flower pattern, a forerunner of what became known as the Kerswell Daisy pattern, and the sgraffito mottoes were written in a childlike handwriting which was often sloping; this pattern was usually covered in a warm honey glaze (see fig. 9). Another early design was of scrolls and zig-zag patterns done in sgraffito and coloured in with blue, green and yellow (the pattern was later given the code Q1) under a clear glaze (see fig. 4). This design

Fig. 3. Reverse of jug seen in fig. 2 decorated with the Kerswell daisy pattern under a warm honey or amber glaze.

Fig. 4. Three examples of early mottowares. The tyg on the left and the two handled jardiniere on the right are both variations of the Q1 pattern; Aller Vale c.1895. The plate was made at Watcombe c.1903. Diameter of plate 8½" (21·7cm).

had a similarity to some of the work done at Bideford in the eighteenth century. Sometimes the sgraffito mottoes were filled in with blue. The Kerswell Daisy and Q1 patterns became popular (especially the Kerswell Daisy) and were produced at Aller for over 20 years. When Aller's first foreman, Mr. William Hart, left to join a new pottery being set up in Exeter (The Exeter Art Pottery) in 1891 he also began to decorate pots in the Kerswell Daisy pattern; many of these bear no backstamp but are easily recognisable to the experienced eye because they are more crudely executed and the style of writing is quite distinctive (see fig. 7).

With the popularity of mottowares, the Aller Vale Pottery began to incorporate sayings into many of their other slipware designs, such as the Persian pattern and bird or flower decorations, and to design new ranges of mottowares. The Watcombe Pottery also saw the opportunity to broaden its market with the "new" wares and they began to make mottowares in the 1890s. The Torquay Terracotta Company does not seem to have followed the fashion, which may explain why they went out of business soon after the turn of the century! The Exeter Art Pottery made mottowares from its inception in 1891. These early mottowares had what the Mayor of Burslem described in 1890 as "a great deal of art merit" but, as the potteries sought to satisfy the public demand for mottoes, so "artistic merit" was sacrificed in favour of simpler styles that could be mass produced by less skilled labour. By the early years of the twentieth century four designs began to emerge that were to take over the mottoware trade; these were Scandy (a kind of Prince of Wales feathers design), Cockerels, Ships, and Cottages. These patterns were made by virtually *all* the South Devon potteries and the Cottages became so popular that to many people "Torquay Pottery" is synonymous with "Cottagewares".

For oh tis the men of Devon
To see them I take delight
To haul and to pull to heave and to pull
And to prove themselves in fight.
Aller Vale

Fig. 5. Early Aller Vale mottoware c.1885–1900. The beaker on the left is decorated with forget-me-nots and butterflies and is an example of the rare H1 pattern. Mug 6" (15cm) tall.

Fig. 6. Aller Vale watering pot, 8" (20·3cm) tall overall c.1885. Decorated in brown, tan, sage green and blue slips under a clear glaze. The decoration is similar to the Kerswell daisy pattern, sgraffito motto filled in with blue.

Come fill me full with liquors sweet
For that is good when friends do meet
But pray take care don't let me fall
Lest you lose your liquor jug and all.
Aller Vale

Our heads cool,
Our feet warm
And a drop of good liquor
To do us no harm.
Watcombe

This jug was made at Longpark
In Torquay by the Sea
May health and happiness be theirs
Whoever drinks from thee.
Longpark

FROM *THE POTTERY GAZETTE*

February 1 1895 — Article entitled "Royalty and Pottery" described a visit made by HRH the Princess Louise, Marchioness of Lorne, to the Aller Vale Pottery in 1894:
The princess ". . . considered that Devonshire sentiment and legend should be more utilized in conventionalized local ornament, saying, "Your pixies (fairies) should be useful to you"; since which time they have become more useful than ever before — as displayed on Dartmoor pitchers by the lads of the Allervale villages. It is but fitting that these sprites, hitherto alone known in the west by the frights they occasion and the mischief they do, should, at the word of a Princess, set themselves to be of some use in the world."

January 1 1904 — describes Hart and Moist:
"They have on show a large number of useful pieces with quaint old-time mottoes and old country sayings written upon them. Sugars and creams, teapots, jugs, candle-sticks, tobacco-jars, bowls, dishes, vases, and many other pieces are shown with these mottoes round them in characteristic lettering. Many of the quotations are purely local, but there are others that have a wide application."

December 1 1906 — describes Hart and Moist, Royal Devon Art Pottery, Exeter:
"Motto ware is a very conspicuous section of their productions, and several new and quaint inscriptions have been added to the already large selection."

September 1 1911 — The Royal Aller Vale and Watcombe Art Potteries:
"Trinket sets, lamp tiles, ash trays, pin trays, pen trays, cups and saucers, teapots, vases etc. are shown in motto ware."

Fig. 7. Examples of mottowares made at the Exeter Art Pottery/Hart and Moist c.1891–1913. The tall tankard has a spurious date 1778. The jug in the middle is decorated with a zig-zag pattern under a thick green glaze. Tall tankard 7½" (19cm).

Come my old friend
And take a pot
But mark now what I say
When thou drinkest
Thy neighbours health
Drink not thine own away.
1778
Hart and Moist

Fig. 8. Advertisement which first appeared in the **Pottery Gazette** in January 1904.

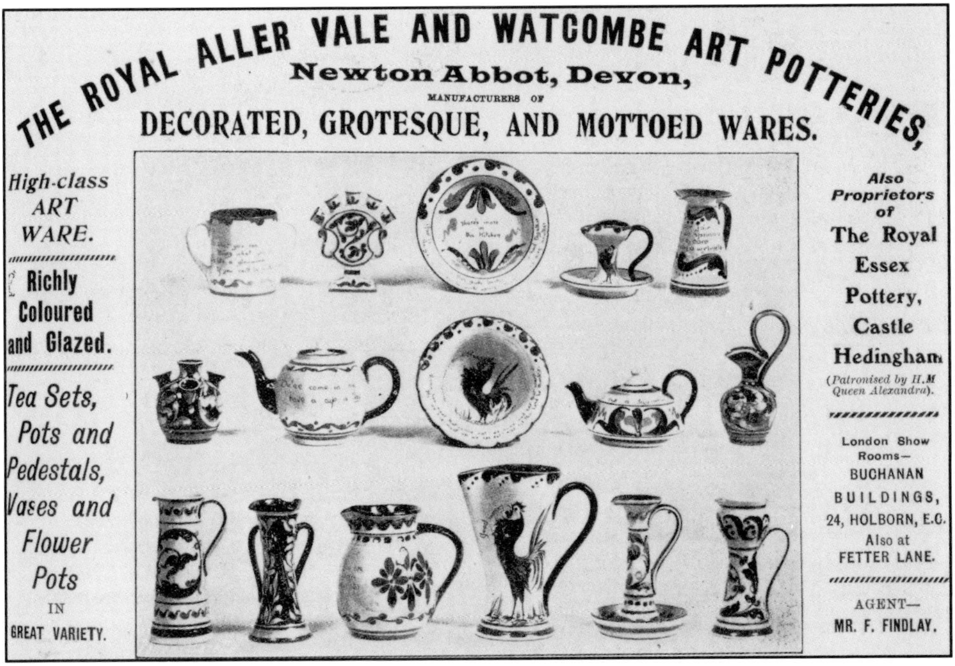

FROM *THE POTTERY GAZETTE*

September 1 1913 — article on "Some South Devon Potteries"

Royal Aller Vale and Watcombe Pottery Co.:

"there is little need, perhaps, to remind the readers of this journal of the scope and the merits of this company's productions, amongst which I think still predominates the quaint and characteristic motto ware for which Devonshire has long been famous. . . . The company's wares are sent out to all parts of England and the Continent, and also to America and the Colonies, which certainly constitutes a testimony to the ability of the Devonshire craftsmen."

May 1 1917 — buyers notes; Royal Aller Vale and Watcombe Art Potteries:

". . . we come to the motto ware, which still has an irrestible attraction for the public, as is proved by its ubiquity in places of popular resort, all up and down the country. Here, again, is a distinct link with the past, for rudely scrawled mottoes were a common characteristic of much of the primitive slip ware. But the art has been worthily and, indeed, nobly developed. In the Aller Vale ware the wording is well chosen, whether it be pithy and humorous sayings, racy of the soil, or proverbs or verses calculated to supply a word in season of encouragement and inspiration; and it is invariably set out in clear and plain characters, easy to be read. The mottoes are applied to vases, large and small, of quaint and pleasing shapes, and also to cruets, butter-dishes, candlesticks, milk jugs, and a variety of useful articles, including some quite recherche trinket sets."

The Popular Mottowares: Scandy, Cockerel, Ship, Cottage

The South Devon potteries were always vieing with each other as to who produced which design *first*! The true facts are probably impossible to ascertain, but from advertisements it would seem that Watcombe and Aller Vale were producing Cockerels and Scandies at the turn of the century and indeed the two companies came under the same ownership in 1901. The Scandy pattern consists of swirling scrolls around a central motif which is similar to Prince of Wales or peacock feathers. The term is thought to have been derived from "Scandinavian" because the design was based (very loosely) on Scandinavian rosemaling. The Ship design followed within the next few years. Hart and Moist (which succeeded the Exeter Art Pottery in 1896) and Longpark made Cockerels, Scandies and Ships c.1904. Hart and Moist would appear to have been the first to introduce the slip decorated Cottage, as they illustrated this in an advertisement in the *Pottery Gazette* in 1912; the other Torquay Potteries did not produce them until c.1915. The Hart and Moist Cottages are very distinctive because they have half timbering on the end wall.

The Scandy pattern

Of the four main designs the Scandy pattern was the most difficult to execute which probably explains why it gradually went out of production in the 1930s. The design varied considerably; earlier examples on large plates, jugs, etc., were often beautifully proportioned with elaborate scrolls around the central motif (see fig. 20). On smaller items the design was often more basic and sometimes the Scandy is so poor that it must have been done by the new boy (or girl!) at the works. The Scandy pattern was normally done in shades of green, blue, yellow, brown and buff on a cream ground, under a clear glaze; this had the pattern code N1. Very occasionally the Scandy pattern appears under an amber glaze — so far, examples of this have been seen from the Aller Vale, Watcombe and Hart and Moist potteries. The Scandy pattern in

Fig. 9 (above). Three examples of the Aller Vale Kerswell daisy pattern. The plate on the right is the earliest, c.1885, and is rather heavily potted; the motto is meant to be read down and up instead of across. The jug and porridge bowl were made c.1905 and the bowl has an appropriate motto from Burns. The "squiggles" either side of "There's mair in the kitchen" are known as "tadpoles" and were common on pieces up to World War I. Height of jug 8¼" (21cm).

Fig. 10 (below). Scandy patterns. The vase with the pinched top was made by Hart and Moist c.1912 and shows the pointed middle "leaf" which was typical of this firm. Other items are Watcombe or Aller Vale. Height of vase: 4½" (11·8cm).

multi-coloured slips was also done on a blue, green or, more rarely, a pink ground — often these colour combinations were over a white clay body so that the sgraffito mottoes appear white instead of the more usual brown. The Watcombe Pottery also decorated pots with a blue slip ground and an all-white Scandy pattern but these are very rare.

Cockerels

The Cockerel pattern originated about the same time as the Scandy and is very popular with collectors today. Cockerels were painted in black, or multi-coloured slips, although they occasionally appear all green or brown; their shape and stance had much more of a "house style" than the Scandy pattern which makes it easier to recognise unmarked examples. Cockerels were a favourite form of decoration throughout the interwar years; after World War II they were continued briefly by Longpark, and the St. Marychurch Pottery also made a few in the 1960s. Generally though, their popularity was overtaken by Ships and Cottages.

Ships

There are probably about as many different types of Ship decoration as there are Potteries that made them! They are usually fishing boats, sometimes referred to as Brixham Yawls although few of them are true Yawls. The earliest ships were usually done in thick brown or buff slip and sailed on a green sea. In the 1920s the Royal Torquay Pottery offered a range of pots decorated with black ships done in pigment — they usually had a pinky coloured sky and a deep peacock blue sea; the mottoes were either sgraffito or painted in black (Watcombe also made a series of rosy sunset pieces but theirs did not carry an inscription, except perhaps, a place name). After World War II, Watcombe modified their ship mottowares so they were much more brightly coloured with a light blue or turquoise sea and a yellow "sunset". They were popular seaside souvenirs throughout the 1950s and many carry the names of holiday resorts.

Vessels large may venture more
Little boats must keep to shore.
Hart and Moist

O Biddiford is ye porte my boy
Of ye maryners bold and trewe
With a heve O ho: have a hoy
When tis Westward of for ye crewe.
Aller Vale

Fig. 11. The ship pattern c.1902–45. Left to right: *Aller Vale jug, Hart and Moist jug, Hele Cross tyg, Longpark coffee pot, Watcombe mug.* In front: *Longpark match striker, ashtray with applied cigarette, unmarked, but probably Royal Torquay. Height of coffee pot 7½" (19cm).*

Fig. 12. Cottages c.1915–62. Left to right, top row: *Babbacombe shaving mug, Watcombe biscuit barrel, Watcombe lamp c.1960 done in brighter colours, Watcombe biscuit barrel, Aller Vale water jug.* Bottom row: *Watcombe plate, Dartmouth cheese or muffin dish, Watcombe jug — cottage with inglenook decorated by Harry Crute, Aller Vale jardiniere, Watcombe plate. Dartmouth ashtray in front. Height of jug: 6½" (16·5cm).*

Cottages

Cottages became the most popular of all the Mottowares and they are still a firm favourite with collectors. There are many different styles of cottage; some enthusiasts have tried to suggest that the decorators based their designs on real cottages, but there seems no firm evidence to support this. Certainly some decorators had their own favourite cottage — for instance, at Watcombe, Bill Critchlow liked to do cottages with a gabled window half way along the front wall and Harry Crute used to put an inglenook chimney on the outside (see fig. 12). Generally, though, the potteries had a "house style" which formed the basic shape for the decorators to copy. The cottages were usually done in a childlike manner — front door in the middle and two windows either side! No attempt was made at realism — sometimes the front door was so tall it reached into the upper floor, other times only a midget could get through it! As the workers were poorly paid and on piece rates this probably accounts for the eratic design. In the 1950s Watcombe introduced a "winter" version of the cottage; this was done on a blue ground and the cottage had snow on its roof and on the ground — next to it stood a fir (or Christmas) tree also covered in snow (see fig. 46).

Fig. 13. Watcombe jardiniere c.1925. 5½" (14cm) tall.

If your not a beauty
Be happy that your plain
Be a wheel greaser
If you can't drive a train.
Aller Vale

He that buys land buys many stones
He that buys flèsh buys many bones
He that buys eggs buys many shells
He that buys ale buys nothing else.
Watcombe

Errors like straws upon the surface glow
He who would seek for pearls
Must dive below.
Longpark

Fig. 14. Variations of the Scandy pattern. The harvest jug was made by Watcombe c.1905. The two water jugs are white clay and were made by Aller Vale c.1900 — the larger one has a Scandy over a khaki ground (S3) and the other is on a dark green ground (S2). The jug shows the Scandy on a blue ground. The plate was made by Daison c.1932 and is done in brighter colours. Harvest jug 7" (17·8cm) tall.

Fig. 15. A variety of cockerels. Large water jug on the left shows the Longpark coloured cockerel; puzzle jug Longpark black cockerel; the coffee pot shows a Watcombe black cockerel. The egg cup is by Hart and Moist; jug inscribed "Paignton" by Royal Torquay; inkwell with coloured cockerel by Aller Vale. The jug at the front inscribed "The Old Smithy" is a very late example of the cockerel pattern, made by the St. Marychurch Pottery c.1963.

From *Brunel's Tower* by Eden Phillpotts Published by Heinemann 1915*

Sometimes came a geat order from Ireland for ware to be sprigged with shamrocks; sometimes Scotland desired "the Cock of the North" on five thousand teapots or ashtrays. . . .

Mr. Marsland, a decorator, described how he did the borders:
" 'Ups and downs' we call this", he said. "Just a row of little twiddles, now up, now down, round the edge of the cup. I put them in like lightening as you see". In a few seconds he had set one and twenty regular splashes round his mug.

Mr. Marsland described the Scandy pattern:
"Spots and streaks and twiddles and the peacock's feather design — all go on with the same ease and swiftness", he explained to Porter. "Seven colours go to each piece, and there are sixty touches of the brush upon each piece. . . . Sometimes on my good days . . . I'll do five and twenty to thirty dozen pieces as this in a day. That's eighteen thousand touches and streaks of colour in eight hours. . . ."

Joanna invented the picture of a boat with a brown sail, floating on a blue sea. This design proved successful beyond expectation; and Mr. Pitts, during a lighter moment, had made a little dish, or ashtray, in the shape of a flat fish. Upon it were written the words "A pla(i)ce for everything", and this joke so pleased the public that the fish was wanted quicker than it could be made. A purple thistle for Scots firms also occupied the new flower-painter, who had succeeded Miss Medway.

* *Brunel's Tower* by Eden Phillpotts was published in 1915; it is a novel set in the Torquay potteries. The title alludes to the Longpark pottery, which occupied buildings previously part of Brunel's atmospheric railway scheme, although the descriptions probably relate to items/incidents at other potteries in the Torquay area as well as Longpark.

The appeal of the mottoes

Whatever the decoration, the appeal of Mottowares was in the Mottoes themselves; especially popular were the "quaint old time mottoes and country sayings". The *Pottery Gazette* noted in 1905:

> "Devonshire and Scotch mottoes are the most popular and are met with away from their place of origin" — and they quoted, as an example, the "especially Devonian motto":
> "Be happy while you're living
> You'll be a long time dead"

"Wind and Dust"
The devil sends the naughty winds
To blow the girls skirts high
But God is just to send the dust
To blind the bad man's eye.
Longpark

When God did guide his sails and course
The winds were at command
And Totnes was the happy shore
When first he came on land.
Aller Vale

"The Old Grandfather's Clock"
Here my master bids me stand
To mark the hours with faithful hand
To do his will is my delight
To serve him well by day and night
Master be wise and learn of me
To serve thy God as I serve thee.
Unmarked

The journey's long from A to Z
And puzzles many a curly head
But leads to books, Red Green or Blue
Which brings the fairy land in view.
Longpark

Words are easy like the wind
Faithful friends are hard to find.
Exeter Art Pottery

The potteries competed with each other to produce new witticisms as these had an irresistible attraction for the public; the Watcombe Pottery went a step further in its quest to give the public what it wanted, and opened a book in which visitors could write their own favourite mottoes. Unfortunately this book "disappeared" when the Pottery closed in 1962.

New potteries were established to make mottowares

Mottowares were so popular that by the time of World War I they were the main output of the Royal Aller Vale and Watcombe Pottery, Hart and Moist, and Longpark. These potteries continued to make other Art Pottery which tended to follow the fashion of the day and was known collectively as "Devonshire Ware" on account of the brown clay. New potteries were established to make Devonshire Ware and Mottowares, e.g. The Royal Torquay Pottery (established on the site of the Torquay Terracotta Company); Tor Vale which evolved into Lemon and Crute (c.1914) and Daison (1926); The Barton Pottery; Plymouth Pottery Company, The Bovey Art Pottery and Devon Tors. The last three are certainly not in the Torquay area although their wares are still recognised by the generic term "Torquay Pottery". Even further afield were the Crown Dorset Pottery at Poole, Wesuma Pottery at Weston-super-Mare and Powell at Buckley, North Wales, who made Torquay style mottowares.

The range of mottowares

The range of wares produced with mottoes was enormous. Most widely produced were the domestic wares such as teapots, sugar bowls, milk/cream jugs, cups and saucers, and plates. Many different shapes and styles were made but the most popular teapot was certainly the squat, angular type given the shape code 1476 — it was produced for over fifty years. The potteries also tried to keep up with changing lifestyles and in about 1950 Watcombe produced a plate with a shallow well at one side for the cup which was known as a "TV Set"; the plate was rimless (an American innovation) and critics claimed the plates would not catch on in Britain because there was nowhere to put the salt! Perhaps this accounts for the relative scarcity of these items today.

The Torquay potteries made other utilitarian items such as Coffee Pots, Cocoa Jugs, Sets of Jugs, Jam/Marmalade/ Honey Jars, Porridge Bowls, Toast Racks, Egg Cups, Condiment Sets, etc. — whatever one might need in the kitchen/dining room was available in mottoware. For the living room there were numerous sizes and styles of plant pots (they were never known as Jardinieres in those days!), Vases, Tobacco Jars and Ashtrays, even Fruit Bowls or Biscuit Barrels — these had appropriate mottoes such as "if you want zum biscuits, 'ere they be". For the desk or writing table there were inkwells and pen trays — in some cases they were combined but these are now quite rare (see fig. 16).

Upstairs, one could adorn the dressing table with a whole variety of items: Dressing Table Trays, Powder and Puff Bowls, Ring Holders, Hatpin Holders or Trays, Candlesticks, Scent Bottles, etc., and for the Washstand or Bathroom there were Shaving Mugs and Soap Dishes. Possibly the potteries even made Washing Sets (Jug and Bowl) and Chamberpots — none of these have been found in mottowares but Royal Torquay made them decorated with Parrots or Fruit; miniature Chamberpots were made and these usually carried the maxim "Morning and Evening exercise".

The popular items of mottowares are still fairly easy to find but collectors should also look for the rarer pieces too, such as a Longpark Bell decorated with a Scandy and the Motto "Bosham Church Oldest Bell 1542" (Babbacombe also made Bells decorated with Cottages); a Hart and Moist Lemon Squeezer or perhaps the model of a Cornish Pasty made by Watcombe — these were made in both Cottage and Scandy designs. Hart and Moist also made Egg Timers but these are very rare. In the 1950s Watcombe made some electric light Lamp bases decorated with Cottages done in brighter colours than was usual; the bases were bottle shaped and rather unstable so they are easily knocked over (and broken) — perhaps this explains why these are scarce today (see fig. 12).

Jist send a line tu lets know ow
Yu'm gwaine on.
Longpark

Fig. 16. Selection of inkwells. The centrepiece is a combined pen tray and inkwell made by Longpark.

Fig. 17. Selection of mottowares made by the Royal Torquay Pottery c.1910–35. The wheelbarrow is a child's toy. The jug at the back is 6½" (16·5cm) tall.

Fig. 18. Contemporary advertisement illustrating popular items with retail prices (catalogue numbers are shown, these are not shape numbers) c.1912.

Fig. 19. Tobacco jars. Left to right: *Watcombe C3 pattern, Hart and Moist, Watcombe. All c.1895–1900. Height of centre jar: 7″ (17·8cm).*

WHOLESALE PRICES

LONGPARK IN THE 1930s

½ pint teapots	10/– dozen
1 pint teapots	16/– dozen
1½ pint teapots	20/– dozen
2 pint teapots	27/– dozen
Teacups and saucers	9/– dozen
Egg cups	4/– dozen
Toast racks (5 bar)	24/– dozen
Shaving mugs	16/– dozen

WATCOMBE IN 1958

6″ Baby plates	45/9 dozen
Cheese dish	81/6 dozen
Cruets on stands	81/6 dozen
Egg cups	18/6 dozen
Toy teapots	41/– dozen
8″ plates	38/9 dozen
1476 teapot, small size	57/– dozen
Toast rack (3 bar)	46/6 dozen

Named ware 5% extra

A pipe lets take
For old times sake.
Aller Vale

The value of tobacco is best understood
When it is the last you puff
And there is no chance of getting more.
Bismark
Hart and Moist

Many a sorrow we forget
Through pipe, cigar or cigarette.
Watcombe

Give every man thy ear
But few thy voice.
Aller Vale

Fig. 20. Selection of items for the dressing table.

The decline of the potteries

The Depression or World War II brought about the decline of many of the old South Devon potteries so that only Longpark and Watcombe survived into the post war world. Longpark closed in 1957 having been bought out by Watcombe, but they too only managed to survive another five years. However, this was not the end of Devon Mottowares because a new pottery had opened at Dartmouth in 1948 and their best known regular line throughout the 1950s was the "Devon Cottage". *The Pottery and Glass Review* of July 1952 remarked of this "it finds a ready sale in the USA and also in Canada and the other Dominions"; this accounts for the availability of this pottery overseas. Dartmouth stopped making mottowares in the early 1960s and now concentrate on slip cast wares. Other Torquay potteries which were set up to make mottowares included the St. Marychurch Pottery, established in 1962 by brothers Cyril and Roy Wilson, ex-Watcombe employees, and Babbacombe Pottery, which made Cottagewares in the 1960s. Mottowares are still being made in the traditional manner by Ron Jackson in South Devon; these are much paler in colour than their earlier counterparts.

SOUTH DEVON POTTERIES

Watcombe Pottery, St. Marychurch, 1869–1962.
Torquay Terracotta Company, Hele Cross, Torquay, 1875–c.1905, reopened as Royal Torquay Pottery Co. to c.1939.
Aller Vale Pottery, Kingskerswell, 1881–c.1924.
Longpark Pottery Co., Newton Road, Torquay, began 1883 as a terracotta company c.1903–1957 Art Pottery and Mottowares.
Exeter Art Pottery, Exeter, 1891–1896, then known as Hart and Moist to 1935.
Tor Vale Pottery, Teignmouth Road, Torquay, c.1913/14; then taken over by Lemon and Crute to 1926; became Daison Art Pottery to c.1932.
Barton Pottery, Torquay, c.1921–39.
Devon Tors Pottery, Bovey Tracey, 1921–
Plymouth Pottery, Plymouth, c.1926–? (short lived).
Bovey Tracey Art Pottery — subsidiary of Royal Torquay in 1930s.
Dartmouth Pottery, 1948–
Babbacombe Pottery, 1952–
St. Marychurch Pottery, 1962–69.

Fig. 21. Watcombe advertising piece for a shop display 3½" (9cm) tall. Cornish pasties also by Watcombe.

If you can't climb — fly.
Longpark

Bearded or shaven
Wit comes from heaven.
Watcombe

Fig. 22. Nightlight holder and shaving mug by Longpark. Nighlight holder 4¾" (12cm) tall.

Unusual Mottowares

Although the four main designs of mottowares were their "Bread and Butter" lines, the South Devon Potteries continually brought out new patterns some of which were produced for only a very short time. The range was so extensive that it is impossible to describe them all; in any case, new patterns continually come to light so no list could claim to be complete. Suffice, then, just to describe a few designs to illustrate the sheer variety to be found.

Around the turn of the century the Watcombe Pottery produced a very delicate scroll design that was given the code C3; it consisted of asymetrical swirls trailed in various coloured slips in a style reminiscent of Scandinavian rose maling. Another contemporary design produced by both Watcombe and Aller Vale was of forget-me-nots done in blue and brown with green leaves; this was developed from a much earlier Aller Vale style known as Majolica. Some pieces also had butterflies added in pink, blue, green and yellow but these are rarely seen (see fig. 5).

Some early twentieth century mottowares were decorated with animals and birds. Aller Vale and Watcombe both made pots with a donkey's or parrot's head; continuing on the animal theme, Longpark produced pots decorated with cows and others with farmyard scenes. Aller, Watcombe and Longpark all made pieces with a chicken hatching from an egg, a Watcombe Porridge Bowl with this decoration had the motto "Don't count your (chicken picture) afore they hatch". Several potteries also made pieces decorated with a cat sitting on a wall; these pieces are remarkably similar in style and offer the possibility that they were done by the same decorator who moved from one pottery to another. Also on a Cat theme were the models of grotesque cats which had mottoes on their bodies; these were made by Aller Vale, Watcombe, Longpark and Tor Vale. A Watcombe example c.1910 has brown and green spots over a cream body and the motto "Has anybody seen our cat" in sgraffito down its back (see fig. 25). Hart and Moist made models of smiling sitting monkeys with "our ancestor" on their backs — these are usually amber glazed.

During the first decade or so of the twentieth century the potteries occasionally added mottoes to their art wares, for instance, vases decorated with daffodils on a dark green ground sometimes had mottoes such as "I cum from Torquay" piped in white slip on the reverse. Dark green was a very fashionable colour in the period up to World War I and in 1911 Watcombe and Aller brought out a new range of plain green wares with white piping mottoes. Today these are less desirable to collectors, probably because of their plainness, although in small items such as Egg Cups they can look quite attractive.

By c.1910 the potteries were giving their mottowares a "regional" flavour by decorating them with thistles or shamrocks and adding an appropriate motto such as "Old Erin's native land"; these patterns were made up until the 1950s so they obviously had wide appeal. More unusual were the mottowares with foreign inscriptions; these were often incorrectly spelt too, which can make translation more difficult. Welsh was probably used more often than any other language and occured as the simple "Bore da" (Good day) or "Hufen da" (Good cream) on jugs. More unusual was the

Fig. 23. Mug with rural scene. Longpark c.1908. Height 3½" (9cm).

Fig. 24. Selection of pots with an animal theme c.1900–1915. Left to right, back row: *Cat and donkey jugs by Watcombe, Tor Vale vase, Aller Vale vase with a scandy pattern sweeping up to dolphins' heads.* Bottom row: *Plate (unmarked) under amber glaze, Watcombe jug with applied mouse, Aller Vale water jug. The cat pieces are all believed to have been decorated by the same artist, probably James Main. Height of scandy vase: 7¾" (20·2cm).*

"Heb dduw heb din" (Without God without anything) on a Longpark Shaving Mug or "Bydd Haelionus Lle Bo Achos" (Be generous where there's cause) on an unmarked Hatpit Holder decorated with ships.

Watcombe also made pots with Gaelic inscriptions e.g. "Maduinn mhath cupan tae" (Good morning cup of tea) and also items with Manx inscriptions such as "Kys ta shin" (Time enough) — these were often decorated with the three legged Isle of Man symbol. Aller Vale made breakfast sets in plain colours with a simple piped inscription "Bon Jour" (the French Good Day).

Before World War I Watcombe began to make pots depicting specific places — Cockington Forge appears to be the earliest — and these continued to be made until the 1950s. More common are Portland Bill, Anne Hathaway's Cottage and the bridge at Bourton on the Water but collectors should look for the rarer Burns Cottage, Lindisfarne or the overseas scenes such as Niagara Falls. In the 1920s and 30s Royal Torquay made a great variety of Jugs, Vases, etc., which depicted named scenes done in relief; these are rather heavily potted and often poorly decorated though.

FROM *THE POTTERY GAZETTE*

July 1 1913 — report of the Ghent Exhibition — the Royal Aller Vale and Watcombe Art Potteries display:

"What Continental customers will make of the dialect mottoes we do not know, but at any rate there is much to attract them in the quaint shapes and usually unassuming decorations of this well-known ware. Among the motto goods I noticed an assortment of useful articles such as candlesticks, butter dishes, egg cups, jugs, etc., but far higher artistic flights have been made in producing many of the art vases. Some of these have been printed with views of Cockington village, the pretty rural street being shown in perspective. Windmills and fishing boats are also used. . . ."

Fig. 25. Winking cats. Left: *Aller Vale cat decorated with moons and stars and painted motto.* Right: *Watcombe cat decorated with brown and green spots and sgraffito motto. In the middle is an Aller Vale dog bowl. Cats 6" (15·3cm) tall.*

Fig. 26 (left). Shamrock tyg by Aller Vale c.1915.

> **FROM *THE POTTERY GAZETTE***
>
> **Royal Longpark Pottery Co.:**
> "The Devonshire mottoware is freely manufactured, and probably represents the principal commodity produced. . . . A shamrock decoration for Ireland, and a thistle decoration for Scotland, have played an important part in the present year's production."

Commemoratives and Advertising Pieces

Commemoratives and Advertising Pieces are specialist subjects in themselves but many mottoware enthusiasts like to have one or two examples to add to their collections.

The earliest known Aller Vale Commemorative was made in 1885 — it was in the Kerswell Daisy pattern and was to commemorate "Gordon of Kartoum" — note the incorrect spelling of Khartoum. One of the endearing aspects of mottowares is that they sometimes have spelling mistakes — decorators were only human after all and at the end of a long day anyone could make a mistake! The Torquay Potteries made Commemoratives for most Royal and State occasions e.g. the Birth of Edward VIII (made by Aller Vale and very rare), all the Coronations, the Abdication, Start of World War I, Peace Settlement, etc. These usually had the name of the town or village that they were made for and sometimes a personal name as well. Regimental pieces were popular too — they were first made in the Edwardian

Fig. 27. Items with a regional flavour: Welsh plate by Longpark, shamrock water jug by Aller Vale, jug inscribed with Scottish motto: "I'll be merry and free be say for naebody" by Royal Torquay; all others by Watcombe. Height of shamrock jug: 7½" (19cm).

era, but after World War II Watcombe made many more; these were painted, though, and not slip as the earlier ones had been — they were liked by US Servicemen.

Commemoratives were also made for a seemingly endless variety of other events ranging from local bazaars e.g. Tygs made by Hart and Moist in 1897 for Chiltern Bazaar, to personal mementoes such as an Ashtray made by Watcombe and inscribed "In memory of Dear Old Devon To Mother from Phil 21.4.21". Many personalised items were made for marriages and christenings; a Hart and Moist Teapot decorated with a horseshoe was inscribed "A present to my sister on the occasion of her marriage June 4th 1906 from Alfred" — similar Cups and Saucers were made to commemorate the christenings of her two sons. Many personalised items were probably made for employees at the potteries. Organisations and associations often commissioned pots to be given away at conferences. A superb example of this was a 12" tall vase decorated with the popular diving kingfisher on a blue ground with a black painted inscription on the reverse "Dalhousie Lodge, No. 860 Ladies Festival 1931" — it was made by Watcombe.

Numerous advertising pieces were made by the Torquay Potteries and many of these were Ashtrays with the names of Hotels, Public Houses, etc. Devon Tors made a series of half pint Mugs which were decorated with Public Houses (see fig. 28); they usually had humorous mottoes, sometimes relating to the owner. More unusual were Jugs advertising whisky e.g. an Aller Vale Scandy Jug with the sgraffito inscription "Drink Carnes Well Matured Spirits". Watcombe made an ashtray advertising "L.O.R. Tweedle & Co. Ltd., Capsule Makers, 297 Goswell Rd, London, EC1" which also carried the motto "Pessimism never paid a dividend"! Perhaps most appropriate of all for mottoware collectors

Fig. 28. Commemoratives and advertising pieces. Left to right: *1902 Coronation beaker by Watcombe, L.O.R. Tweddle ashtray by Watcombe, RAMC (Royal Army Medical Corps) jug unmarked, Keigwin Arms jug by Devon Tors, miniature tyg to commemorate the entry of the USA into World War I in 1917 by Hart and Moist, Ladies Festival ashtray by Babbacombe, Dreadnought whiskey jug by Watcombe, Foxhunters Inn mug by Devon Tors.*

are the pieces advertising the potteries themselves — Watcombe and Longpark definitely made them but they are very rare yet many must have been made for the shops that sold the pottery (see fig. 21).

COMMEMORATIVES

May they ever be united,
Our hearts our hopes,
Our prayers our tears,
Our faith triumphant o'er our fears
Are all with thee.
Hart and Moist/Aller Vale

Britannia mourns her heroes now at rest,
Each of them doing their Country's work. (Boer War).
Aller Vale

We therefore have great cause of thankfulness 1937 VR 1897.
Aller Vale

Freely drink and quench thy thirst
Here drank the Pilgrim Fathers first.
Aller Vale

ADVERTISING

Freyland Ale — Whenever I drink of Freyland Ale
Drawn from an old brown bottle,
I feel as if a summer morn
Was running down my throttle —
(Ammon Wrigley)
(R.Torquay)

R.S.G.B. CONVENTION/BRISTOL/ SEPT. 1954
Radio Society of Great Britain.
(Cottage plus TV aerial)

BID CORONATION CONFERENCE FOLKESTONE 1953
(British Industries Distributors)

ROSLYN HALL HOTEL/TORQUAY/ TEL. 4373.

CLAY CONVENTION 1959 TORQUAY
(All four above Watcombe)

GOLFERS' LIQUEUR WHISKEY — Sir J. Caust & Sons Ltd., London.
(Unmarked)

HOW TO IDENTIFY AND DATE MOTTOWARES

IT was the basic policy of the potteries to mark their wares with their factory of origin but many pieces "escaped" this process, probably because of the necessity to speed up the production line and also because workers were paid at piece rates; there are many stories from old potters of how they used to "fiddle" the number of pots they had decorated or marked to keep their wages up! Collectors like to know the attribution of their pots and much of the skill of identification comes with experience. However, for the beginner, there are a number of "pointers" as to source of pottery and its date; it is important to realise that these are "pointers" and not definite identification because the only thing one can be definite about is that there are *always* exceptions to the rules! When trying to identify an unmarked pot it is necessary to look at *all* its features i.e. the design, colours, glazes, lettering and the type of clay used and then come to an overall assessment of its likely source.

1. The basic decoration. It is only with the popular mottowares that it is possible to make generalisations about style; unusual pieces were often the work of an individual potter and he or she may well have taken their decoration from one pottery to another.

(a) The Scandy pattern. Generally speaking, it is not possible to identify unmarked pots purely from the style of Scandy because they vary so much. However, if the Scandy has a pointed middle "feather" or "spear" then it almost definitely comes from Hart and Moist although not all their Scandies have a pointed middle (see fig. 29). More elaborate Scandies are probably early — i.e. before c.1915.

(b) Cockerels. Cockerels have much more of a "house style" than the Scandy pattern (see fig. 15). Aller Vale Cockerels are usually coloured (done in green/blue/brown and black slips) although they also decorated some that were all black; they are usually standing very proudly with their heads well back, obviously crowing loudly! Their tail feathers are also held high, and these are rather "spikey". Watcombe Cockerels are usually black and their heads are upright; sometimes their legs are set apart almost as though dancing, and they usually stand in thick green grass. Watcombe occasionally made coloured, brown or even green Cockerels but these are often of poor quality. Longpark made both black and coloured Cockerels in great quantity; they tend to be upright but very full breasted birds. Hart and Moist Cockerels are also plump breasted but they taper down to rather a thin rump end and their tails are short and limp; they are normally black and stand amongst spiky sgraffito grass. Watcombe and Hart and Moist birds often have "Good Morning" issuing form their beaks. Other Torquay potteries also decorated with Cockerels, even as late as the 1960s at the St. Marychurch Pottery,

Fig. 29. The Hart & Moist Scandy pattern.

but these are fairly unusual so it is not possible to discern common features.

(c) Ships. The Ship decoration varied considerably even within the same pottery so generalisations are difficult. Most of the Ships done up to World War II had brown sails but if the sails are a paler buff to tan colour then the pot is likely to be Longpark. After World War II Watcombe produced a range of Ships that were more brightly coloured with turquoise or bright blue sea and often a yellow sunset; these are very distinctive.

(d) Cottages. The Cottage design was the most widely produced of all the mottowares (see fig. 30). Aller and Watcombe Cottages are usually two storey, although sometimes a "bungalow" crops up, often on a squat item where there isn't space for two storeys. Longpark Cottages are invariably single storey and their outlines are much thicker than Watcombe or Aller. Of the other potteries there are a few generalisations that can be made: Babbacombe Cottages are of very good quality, especially in the glazing, and they have two or three birds in the sky. If a Cottage has blue windows it is most likely to be Dartmouth, although not all Dartmouth Cottages were done in this way. Hart and Moist Cottages have exposed timbers on the end wall and steeply pitched roofs — however, the Plymouth and Crown Dorset Potteries also made similar Cottages so this feature is not a definitive point of identification.

2. Borders. Borders, decorative edging and motifs can be of great help when trying to date a piece of pottery; in general, the more decoration the earlier the pot is likely to be. Up until World War I it was common for Scandy and Cockerel pots to have borders of green or blue swirls interspersed with dots either painted directly onto the cream ground or on a wide band of colour slip (see fig. 20); this type of border occurs on Aller Vale, Watcombe, Longpark and Hart and Moist pottery. Another feature of this period was a motif shaped like a swimming tadpole which was used to fill up empty areas at the side of Scandy decorations, or on other patterns such as the Kerswell

Fig. 30. Different styles of cottage pattern. Biscuit barrel and large jug by Watcombe; matchstrikers: rear Aller Vale, front, Longpark; small jug and muffin dish by Devon Tors; ashtray by Babbacombe; egg cup by Dartmouth. Height of biscuit barrel 6½" (16·9cm).

Daisy (see fig. 31). These tadpoles occur in any colour slips and were used up until c.1918. A variation of this was a row of overlapping elongated tadpoles usually done in green and supposed to represent seaweed; this was first introduced at the turn of the century but continued to be used up until World War II (see fig. 31).

A more simple border decoration consisted of a row of dots or a plain band of colour; blue was more common, although green was also used. On later pieces, especially those made after World War II, the dots are widely spaced (to save time) or in some cases the borders have been abandoned altogether. If the dots are large and are shaped to look more like commas then the pot is more likely to be Longpark, although some Watcome and Royal Torquay pots were decorated in this way too (see fig. 32).

3. Colours and Glazes. On earlier twentieth century slip decorated mottowares the colours are more muted than later wares, and it is likely that several different colours will have been used, perhaps five or six colours on a Scandy for instance. During the inter war years the colours were brighter and applied more thinly; the Daison Art Pottery used a very bright blue on their Scandies in the early 1930s. Another distinctive feature of Daison was their tendency to use black on the reverse of the rims of plates etc.

The glazes also affected the colour of decoration. Early glazes contained lead and this gave a warm glow to the pots; in the 1950s lead glazes were banned for domestic wares and the new glazes made the pots much whiter and the colours were brighter. The quality of the glazing can also help to identify unmarked pottery. Lemon and Crute/Daison and Barton always used top quality glazes and their pots appear very shiny and evenly glazed. At the other end of the scale, the Royal Torquay Pottery used poor glazes so their pots are often found with cracked or chipped glazing. Royal Torquay tried to economise in production by only firing the pots once and this led to rather poor quality wares which have suffered badly from the ravages of time.

Fig. 31. Tadpole motif on hat pin holder, seaweed design and "commas" or dots around top of jug.

Fig. 32. The strong distinctive lettering of Longpark Pottery, and comma border.

Collectors may sometimes find pots where the colours have run and gone streaky; this is usually caused by faulty firing causing the pot to become overheated.

4. Lettering and Dates. The inscriptions on Mottowares were either done by scratching the messages through the slip base, or by a piping technique, or by painting over the slip; some very late pieces of Watcombe have been seen with transfer printed place names over the glaze but these may have been done by the retailer rather than the pottery. Of these methods, it is the sgraffito inscriptions that are the most distinctive and can be used to identify the source of unmarked pottery.

On very early Aller Vale pots the inscriptions are crudely done and vary considerably; this was probably because the decorators did their own inscriptions

Fig. 33. The backward sloping lettering of Exeter Pottery.

and many of these were still learning their crafts at the Cottage Art Schools. The lettering often slopes and is sometimes filled in with blue, although Longpark are also known to have used a blue infill in the 1920s.

On the popular Mottowares, Aller Vale and Watcombe inscriptions are very similar, the lettering is sturdy and well rounded. A few early examples also have very elaborate capital letters, although these are quite rare.

Most Longpark lettering is very distinctive because it was done with a broad based instrument (e.g. a very blunt nail) which produced thick lines (see fig. 32); the letter "e" is often quite curly and was the speciality of one of their motto writers, Mr. Len Mayo.

Exeter Art Pottery/Hart and Moist lettering is invariably sloping backwards and on many pieces the letters are poorly formed which can make them difficult to decipher especially if the motto is in dialect (see fig. 33). Another feature of these firms was that many of their early mottowares incorporate spurious dates such as "1679" or "1815" etc., the reason for these dates is unknown except perhaps their desire to recreate pottery on ancient traditional lines (see fig. 7). However, if collectors see unmarked pots which have all the hallmarks of Exeter pottery but carry these early dates then do not be put off by the dates. Apart from some examples of the Exeter potteries, all other Torquay pottery which has an incised date is most likely to be contemporary with the pot.

5. Clay. Having looked at the decoration and lettering on the pot, the next thing to do is to examine the clay. Some books and articles on Torquay pottery have claimed that it is possible to positively identify pots from the colour of the clay but there is very little evidence to support this. Early Aller Vale is often very red, but then so is some Watcombe and also Plymouth pottery. The colour of the clay is partly dependent on its original composition when dug, but also on mixing at the pottery and the temperature at which it is fired; a higher temperature produces a darker finish. The only

O list to me ye Ladies fair
And when ye wish to curl your hair
For the safety of this domicile
Pray place your lamps upon this tile
Many hands make light work
Take a little Toast
Have courage boys to do the right
Be bold, be brave, be strong,
By doing right you gain the might
To overcome the wrong
Full many a shaft at random spent
Finds mark the Archer never meant
And many a word at random spoken
Can wound or heal a heart thats broken

To teach his grandson draught
His leisure hed employ
Until at last the old man
Was beaten by the boy
only stand and wait
A place for everything
And everything in its place
Full many a shaft at random sent
Finds mark the Archer never meant
And many a word at random spoken
Can wound or heal a heart thats broken
Muffin's Muggin's
Boscastle

definite pointer based on the clay is that if it appears to contain very fine particles of grit then it is likely to be Hart and Moist.

Most of the clays used were dug locally although the seams varied considerably. The red clays came from Torquay, Exeter or Plymouth areas and these were either used on their own or mixed with white clay which came from the Teign valley. White clay was also used on its own especially by Aller Vale although Watcombe, Hart and Moist and Longpark are also known to have used it. Aller Vale also mixed some red with white to produce a pinky coloured clay. White and pink clays were used prior to World War I and were usually dipped in dark slips with the mottoes scratched into the white body. The Watcombe Pottery experimented with white clay c.1960 shortly before they closed; although, so far as is known, they did not used it for traditional mottowares.

6. Marks/Backstamps etc. on Pottery. The potteries used a great variety of marks to identify their pottery; a very small selection of these is shown in this booklet. For a more comprehensive list collectors are recommended to obtain the Torquay Pottery Mark Book (available from TPCS); this contains over 130 marks from all the South Devon Potteries plus some marks of other Torquay style wares and names of known outlets. Sometimes Torquay pottery is only marked with the name of an outlet e.g. "Middletons China Stores, Newton Abbot" or "Made for Herberts".

Other marks on the base of pots are likely to be pattern codes and shape numbers and these are scratched or painted. The pattern codes relate to the decoration and they consist of a letter and a number e.g. N1 which is a Scandy pattern on a cream ground. Pattern codes were first used at Aller Vale but were copied by the other major potteries. Occasionally pots are discovered which have the wrong pattern code, presumably because they were allocated to one design but then were hastily decorated in another pattern to meet a rush order. Pattern codes appear on pots from about 1890 to the early twentieth century. Shape

> ***Hope for the best, look for the best***
> ***The worst will never appear,***
> ***Pray for the best then leave the rest***
> ***God always answers a prayer.***
> ***Longpark***

numbers usually consist of three or four numbers; they were first used at Aller in the 1890s but continued to be used, albeit intermittently, throughout the interwar years. Most of the potteries seem to have developed their own shape numbers. Some very early examples of mottoware from the Aller Vale Pottery are only marked with a "potters mark" — these are very small impressed symbols such as a letter T or a Crescent; for more information consult the Torquay Pottery Mark Book.

Having gone through the list of "pointers" the collector should now have a reasonable idea of the source of an unmarked pot. In some cases though, mysteries remain mysteries even to the very experienced collector. The only way to become more skilled at identification is to look at (and feel!) as many pots as possible and to compare unmarked pots with marked examples. Good hunting.

Fig. 34. Well marked example of an unglazed or dry base on a Aller Vale pot.

LOOKING AT BOTTOMS . . . of pots, of course!

IT was the general policy of the Torquay potteries to mark their mottowares with their factory of origin. However, even the beginner will soon discover that many pots have very indistinct marks or perhaps no marks at all. This can normally be explained by human error or speed of production. The pottery workers were paid on piece rates and many of them have related how they used to slip in a few unstamped pots to keep their numbers (and wages) higher. On other occasions, if the conveyor belt system got a "jam" then pots would be rushed through without marking — especially if the kilns were waiting to be filled.

Most collectors like to know the attribution of their pots and to understand what the various numbers and figures mean. The examples illustrated in figs. 34 & 35 are typical of the bases of well marked pots.

Fig. 34. Aller Vale pot. The Aller Vale mark has been impressed using a backstamp which was often made of metal or even pottery. This stamp was used from the mid-1880s to about 1893, and the dry base of the pot is also typical of early wares. The incised number 154 refers to the shape of the pot; shape numbers are usually three or four digits, presumably higher numbers indicate a later shape although as yet very little research has been done on the classification of shape numbers so this is speculation! Occasionally shape numbers are found which could possibly be interpreted as dates, for instance, a Watcombe vase with 1948 on the base. However, there is no evidence at all that any of the numbers on the bases of mottoware pots were dates — the example mentioned, 1948, was slip decorated with heather on a dark green ground which was typical of the Edwardian period. The incised I4 was the decoration code which indicated the Kerswell Daisy pattern.

Fig. 35. Well marked example of a glazed base on a Longpark pot.

Fig. 35. Longpark pot. this is an example of a pottery mark which has been done using a black rubber stamp; this mark was used from about 1904 to the end of World War I. The shape number, 313, and the decoration code, N1 (the scandy pattern), have both been painted using black paint. The base of the pot has been glazed and the three little white dots in the shape of a triangle were made by the fire-clay stilts which supported the pot during firing.

Complete sets of marks such as in these examples are indicative of early pots made before the 1920s. During the interwar years the shape numbers and pattern codes were gradually dropped, although they continued to be used in the catalogues.

Often the marks on pots are very indistinct and can cause great frustration to the collector who is anxious to know their attribution. Turning the pot in a good light can sometimes reveal letters more clearly, as can breathing on the pot, or even placing it under water. Magnifying glasses can also be helpful. However, collectors must be careful not to "see" the marks they *want* to see rather than those that are actually there!

SELECTION OF BACKSTAMP MARKS

Aller Vale Pottery

Aller Vale
Devon

Incised. Devon sometimes omitted. 1895–1902.
Black painted. 1902–c.1924.
Black painted with "England" or "made in England" instead of "Devon". c.1902–1924.

ALLER
VALE
H,H& Co.

Impressed. Used when the pottery was acquired by Messrs Hexter, Humpherson & Co. c.1897–1902.

ALLER
VALE
DEVON
ENGLAND

Impressed. "England" added with a separate stamp. c.1891–1902.

Hart and Moist, Exeter

H.M. EXETER

Impressed. c.1900–

Royal Torquay Pottery

HELE CROSS
POTTERY
TORQUAY

Rubber stamp. 1905–1918.

ROYAL
TORQUAY
POTTERY
ENGLAND

Rubber stamp. 1924–1940.

Longpark Pottery

TORMOHUN
WARE
TORQUAY

Impressed. c.1903–1914.

LONGPARK
TORQUAY
ENGLAND

Black rubber stamp. c.1930–1940 and 1947–1957.

Watcombe Pottery

Incised or painted. Torquay or Torquay, England sometimes added in similar script. c.1901–1920.

Rubber stamp. c.1918–1927.

Black rubber stamp. c.1935–1962.

Devon Tors, Bovey Tracey

Impressed. Bovey or the letter "B" sometimes added. 1920–1939.

Babbacombe Pottery

Black rubber stamp. c.1952

St. Marychurch Pottery

Rubber stamp. 1964–1968.

Dartmouth Pottery

Black rubber stamp. 1948.

Pattern Codes used on Mottowares

A1 Persian pattern on a cream ground.

C2 Stylised forget-me-nots on a cream ground.

C3 Modified rosemaling pattern on a cream ground, believed to be exclusive to Watcombe.

C4 Parrot's head on cream ground.

C5 Donkey's head on cream ground.

H1 Forget-me-nots and butterflies on a cream ground.

I4 Kerswell Daisy pattern under an amber glaze.

K6 Plain green ground with piping inscription.

N1 Scandy pattern on cream ground.

N2 Coloured cockerel on a cream ground.

N3 Black cockerel on a cream ground.

Q1 Sgraffito patterns filled in with coloured pigments on a cream ground.

S1 Scandy on a blue ground.

S2 Scandy on a green ground.

S3 Scandy on a khaki ground.

S4 Scandy on a pink ground.

Y1 Partially dipped items with sgraffito motto.

Fig. 36. The Watcombe C3 pattern.

C3 PATTERN

THE cup and saucer illustrated above are decorated with the pattern given the code C3 and, as far as is known, this decoration was only used at Watcombe. This pattern was introduced at the end of the 1890s and it was only made for a short time. Items that have been seen with this decoration include teapots, jugs, sugar basins and cups and saucers; it was also used for tobacco jars (see fig.19). Almost always the pots have been made from thinner clay than was usual and this gives them a more delicate appearance.

The C3 pattern was based on Scandinavian rosemaling and was one of the precursors of the scandy pattern; the scrolls on the cup have similarities to the outer "wings" of the ornate scandy patterns of the early twentieth century. Many of the old potters believed the term "scandy" to be a derivative of "Scandinavian" although there is no definite proof of this.

Pattern codes were first introduced in the 1890s at Aller Vale as a form of shorthand for the standardised patterns. The same pattern codes were later adopted by some of the other potteries, notably Watcombe and Longpark. The codes have been the subject of much speculation amongst collectors because there seems to be no "logic" to the system. For instance, why is it that the scandy pattern on a cream ground has the code N1 whilst scandy on a green ground is S2? One suggestion is that the letter code denoted a particular designer so that, for instance, all the C patterns were originated by one designer even though they may be executed by various decorators.

Sometimes pots are found which have the "wrong" code for their decoration. The purpose of the codes was to tell the decorators which pattern to use and if a rush order came in some pots might have to be hastily decorated with a different pattern to meet the order. In some cases it could be simply human error! The codes continued to be used as shorthand for ordering pots form the companies' catalogues certainly up until World War Two even though they were no longer marked on the pots themselves.

Gold and goods
May be lost
A good name
Endures for ever.
Hart and Moist

A fool or so from any quarter
May lead a horse or so to water
But 20 men can't make him drink.
Aller Vale

Only the actions of the just
Smell sweet
And blossom in the dust.
1778
Hart and Moist

No place on earth so pleases me
As dear old Torquay by the sea.
Longpark

Make new friends
But keep the old
The first is silver
The second gold.
Watcombe

HINTS WHEN BUYING MOTTOWARES

COLLECTORS are always anxious to know they are buying wisely and one of the questions frequently asked is "What is the right price for a teapot, or a puzzle jug, or an inkwell?" etc. But, given the wide variety of mottowares, a price guide is an impossibility. For a start, prices vary from one part of the country to another, Torquay being one of the more expensive areas. There is more pottery available in South Devon but a lot more collectors are after it too! Prices in America and Australasia are even higher. From reading this book and looking around antique fairs, collectors will learn what is common and what is rare and prices will usually reflect this — unless, of course, an elusive "bargain" turns up. For example, a rectangular pin/ash tray with a cottage or scandy decoration is quite common and should cost only a few pounds; the same decoration with a personalised inscription will roughly double its price, as will a decoration of Shakespeare's House or The Needles, Isle of Wight. However, the same tray with applied medallion heads for the 1935 Silver Jubilee will be likely to cost four or five times the price of a cottage version.

Collectors should learn to decide what they are prepared to pay for a pot and this will be based on what they specialise in. A 1476 cottage teapot incised "From Skegness" will obviously be worth a lot more to a collector of "Skegness" souvenirs than someone only interested in collecting cottage teapots. Really unusual items such as a Cornish pasty or an advertising piece are always worth buying even if the price seems inflated — it may be five years before another one turns up.

Whatever the item, collectors should always examine it carefully for damage, restoration or repairs because this will affect its value. Everyone wants to have perfect pieces but Torquay pottery chips fairly easily so many pieces do have some damage. Some mottowares are now a hundred years old and are bound to show signs of age such as crazing in the glazes. Similarly, a shaving mug bought in the 1920s and used for twenty or thirty years will show some evidence of this.

Look carefully at rims and other edges of pots for signs of damage or repair, check handles to see if they have been off and stuck on again. Teapot spouts are very vulnerable, not least because they were often in everyday use, so look for "chibbles" around the edges. Be sure to look for hairline cracks — these are often difficult to see if the light is poor so, if in doubt, take the piece to window and turn the pot slowly in the light. Small hairline cracks don't matter too much, but they might spread and a "cobweb" of cracks could mean the pot has received a heavy knock and will be weakened. Look carefully at glazes too, especially if the pot is a vase or jardiniere and has been used. Sometimes, if a pot had a minor flaw in the original glaze, water seeps into the pot from the inside and causes the outside glaze and slips to flake off; beware of these because this problem is very difficult to "cure" and, in reality, only completely re-glazing it will stop further flaking.

Collectors should examine "sets" to see that they match and to check that lids and covers are present and correct. The clay used in the Torquay potteries varied considerably so that sometimes lids are a different colour from their accompanying pot, or cheese dish covers are of different clay from the base. This does not matter (except that most collectors would *prefer* items to be of the same colour clay) because the wares were probably sold like that originally. When items such as teapots were made, the bodies of the pots would be made by a thrower, spouts and handles would be moulded separately and lids would be made by another thrower. Therefore, all the parts could easily be made of different batches of clay and would come up in different shades. However, although the clay may not match, the decoration and colours used on separate pieces certainly *should* match. Cottageware teapots never had plain brown lids!

Sometimes pots have been restored and it is very hard to detect. Reputable dealers will always tell customers about restoration or repairs (and faults) — after all, they want your custom again and no-one likes to feel they have been cheated.

All damage, repairs and restoration (no matter how well done) devalues pots but these are still worth buying if the price is right, especially for unusual pieces. Small chips, hairline cracks or excellent restoration will reduce the price by only a small amount, but for large chunks out of a pot or missing lids and covers the price should drop by about a third. Very badly damaged pieces are not worth buying unless they are at "knock down" prices or very rare. The cost of having restoration work done professionally is quite expensive because of the time involved, but many collectors like to do some restoration themselves and this can add an extra dimension to their hobby.

Life were not worth the living,
If no one were the better,
For having met you on the way,
And known the sunshine of your stay.
Aller Vale

Life is a struggle not a race,
A wise man keeps an even pace
Aller Vale

Life is mostly froth and bubble,
Two things stand as stone,
Kindness in another's trouble,
Courage in your own.
Longpark

Life is an echo, it all comes back,
The good, the false, the true,
So give from your heart, the best you can,
And the best will return to you.
Longpark

COLLECTING AND DISPLAYING MOTTOWARES

COLLECTORS enjoy showing off items that they are proud to own — there is little satisfaction in building up a collection only to keep it hidden away in boxes! Giving some thought to what you collect and to its presentation will be worthwhile, both for your own enjoyment and that of your family and friends.

A collection of mixed mottowares from Devon is a pleasure to have, hold and look at, but often there is a desire to specialise and this will be a very personal choice. Collectors may decide to concentrate on just one of the factories e.g. Aller Vale or Watcombe, or to collect only one decoration, such as cottages, from all the factories. Others might be attracted to a particular item such as hat pin holders or puzzle jugs and build up a collection of these. Other possibilities are choosing a colour theme, such as amber glazes, or to concentrate on the mottoes themselves, perhaps collecting just Shakespeare quotations or patriotic mottoes.

Whatever the collection, its presentation will either enhance or detract from it! Choosing the most suitable aids to display and the arrangement of a collection is all important to its enhancement. A varied collection of mottowares can look most attractive displayed in profusion on a pine kitchen dresser (see centre spread), but a rare or particularly fine piece, such

Fig. 37. Selection of pots with a bird theme. Top: *porridge bowl with owl decoration, unmarked but probably Hart and Moist; tyg by Aller Valer, c.1895.* Middle: *two porridge bowls by Watcombe c.1905–10; scent bottle by Longpark c.1930, decorated with a kingfisher on a blue ground.* Front: *inkwells by Royal Torquay; jug with black swan by Watcombe; jug depicting "Old Irish Cock-fight" also by Watcombe c.1910.*

as the Persian pot in fig. 1 deserves to be seen alone to be fully appreciated. Shelving, the mainstay of most collections, will be to one's taste, pocket or availability but shelf size should be matched to the pottery — e.g. small items on light weight units, large items on heavier shelves or furniture with space around them. Glass fronted cabinets save on dusting. Mirror backed shelf units allow mottoes to be shown forward-facing while the pattern on the reverse will be reflected and seen.

Plates, trays, tiles etc. can be fixed to walls — always use plastic covered plate hangers which are the correct size to avoid damage to rims. Wall displays always look better if the walls are plain coloured (choose a colour to complement your collection) and if the items are positioned so that there is symmetry and harmony between them. Plate stands, which are available in plastic, wood or wire, will allow plates to be shown on furniture and shelves; they can also be used to give height to a display.

Many mottoware pieces can be placed informally in appropriate settings e.g. a dressing table set in the bedroom or shaving mugs in the bathroom. Whenever possible use various items to embellish or emphasise the original use of the pottery, for instance, dried flowers in vases, hat pins or matches in holders and candles in candelsticks or holders. Another idea is to make a focal point of your collection by creating a display around it e.g. the dolls tea party in fig. 39 or a Christmas decoration using holly pieces. Framed photos of potters at work or old pottery adverts will make for additional interest to the collection.

Your collection deserves to be presented in the best possible way. It is a good investment, but better still, the mottoes will provide a store of humour, wisdom, and occasionally debate, which will be a talking point for family and visitors alike. Your collection and your hobby should then give you years of pleasure and satisfaction.

MINIATURES AND CHILDREN'S WARES

MINIATURES are fun! Miniatures are usually thought of as very small replicas of larger items; in thinking of them as being around two inches in height collectors are bound to have a few exceptions to the rule, especially if the original large item was tall and thin!

There were very many miniatures made in a great variety of materials — and not a great deal published on the subject!

The Torquay Potteries made miniature candlesticks, chambersticks, vases, tygs, tankards, Toby jugs, plates, commemoratives, animals, birds, teapots, cups and saucers, dolls teasets, matchholders and many other items including terracotta plaques, anything in fact that had been produced in a larger size.

Aller Vale miniatures tended to be mostly decorated with flowers and scroll patterns, although Scandy was done and mottowares produced. Watcombe miniatures varied from terracotta produced around the turn of the century to numerous cream jugs with a motto, e.g. "To thine own self by true", or "Elp yoursel to craim", mostly they have a place name to remind the owner of a holiday memory. These small jugs may well also have been used to provide the individual milk or cream portion on a tray of tea in teashops.

The place names vary from seaside and inland towns in England, Scotland, Wales and Ireland to places as far away as Canada, Australia, New Zealand, South Africa and the U.S.A., so this gives an idea of how far afield the Devon wares travelled and the countries to which they were supplied. A lot of these pieces have mottoes in various dialects from Scottish to Maori — so very often it is necessary to

Fig. 38 (above right): Selected items from a collection of miniatures. Fig. 39 (below right): Dolls teaset by Watcombe; miniature vase by Longpark. In the 1930s Longpark 7-piece dolls teasets sold to retailers at 30/- (£1.50) per dozen sets.

always help a lame dog over a stile
Du all the gude yu kin In every wey yu kin
Clovelly

Jack and Jill
Mary had a little lamb
For My Dolly

Fig. 40. Selection of items made for children. Marjorie Garvey christening plate 7in (17·8cm) diameter; miniature jugs 1¾in (4.5cm).

find a translation for them. The Welsh mottoes appear to be actual Welsh mottoes as against English ones translated into Welsh, and this also applies to the Scottish ones.

It would appear that around 1912 Longpark was the main manufacturer of miniatures, and these were executed with a great deal of skill and detail, especially the decorative plates with their pointed edges and moulded rope pattern around the central motto; these were copying wares made a great deal earlier by ceramic manufacturers. Their very tiny cockerels and Scandies were also of very high quality on the miniature candlesticks, bearing in mind that the decoration had to be executed whilst going around in a circle — no mean feat.

Aller Vale, Longpark and Watcombe and other potteries made miniature teasets. Aller Vale seen to have made the smallest with the teapot only one and half inches high. All these potteries also made dolls' teasets which had various patterns on them, e.g. Scandy, cottage, boats, shamrock, Kingfisher, green, blue and the rare pink glaze. The set should consist of a teapot, jug and sugar basin, two plates, two cups and two saucers. Both the round shape teapot and the 1476 shape teapot were made. Mottoes on these wares varied from "Tak a cup o Tay", "For My Dolly", to nursery rhymes like Jack and Jill, Little Tommy Tucker, Simple Simon met a Pieman going to the Fair, etc.

Hart & Moist, Exeter, also made miniatures in the Scandy and amber glaze, although these are not so plentiful, nor so well done.

Royal Torquay made toys as well as miniatures, e.g. wheelbarrow, boats etc. and these often came in the rosy Sunset Pattern (see fig. 17). Although these are interesting pieces they are rather crudely executed and do not compare to the quality of some of the other Torquay miniatures.

Aller Vale and Watcombe also made miniature artefacts, e.g. The Olde Romsey Bushel 1792, similar to those small porcelain models bearing a hand-painted transfer of a town's coat of arms, which were produced by W. H. Goss and Crested China manufacturers around the 1900s as holiday souvenirs.

Collecting miniatures is a fascinating study in itself and very rewarding — it is now increasing rapidly as houses and homes become somewhat smaller and the space that can be allocated to hobbies becomes reduced accordingly.

Children's ware

Various items were produced for children, for instance, a plate for baby was very popular in the 1920s and 1930s with mottoes or a pattern on the inside of the plate, so that children were encouraged to eat their food to see the writing or the pattern under the meal and thereby finish their dinner to mother's satisfaction.

Other pieces were produced such as egg cups, plates, cups and saucers etc. with names and dates inscribed, probably to commemorate birthdays, christenings, coming of age and other family celebrations as presents from fond grandparents, aunts, godmothers, parents to celebrate a milestone in the child's life. Longpark also made mugs with the inscription For a Good Girl, and For a Good Boy, once again probably as an incentive for relations to take one home for a child when visiting the Potteries whilst on holiday. After all people still do it today — bring something home for the child in the family.

Rosey Posey at five takes Tea,
Dolls and kittens invited free.

To teach his grandson draughts,
His leisure he'd employ,
Until at last the old man,
Was beaten by the boy.

My fairest child, I have no song to give you,
No lark could pipe to skies as dull and grey,
Yet ere we part, one lesson I can leave you,
For every day, Be good sweet maid and let who will be clever,
Do noble things, not dream them all day long,
And so make life, death and that vast forever,
One grand sweet song!

All three above Longpark

A PLA(I)CE FOR ASHES

". . . Mr. Potts, during a lighter moment had made a little dish, or ashtray, in the shape of a flat fish. Upon it were written the words 'A pla(i)ce for everything', and this joke so pleased the public that the fish was wanted quicker than it could be made."

THIS was how Eden Phillpotts described the origins of the little fish shaped ashtray in "Brunels Tower"; it certainly did become very popular and was produced for over 20 years. A Longpark catalogue of the 1930s lists them priced as 5/6 a dozen. Longpark may have originated the design but they were copied by other potteries too — examples have been seen from Watcombe and Royal Torquay. Some of the Royal Torquay fish trays were made by converting a teaplate; these are easy to distinguish because they have a round foot rim on the bottom whereas those made in a fish shaped mould always have an oval foot rim, or a flat oval base.

Scandies and cottages are the most common decorations on the fish trays but other patterns that have been seen include a thistle, and a sailing boat by Longpark and a rosy sunset by Royal Torquay. Almost always the mottoes are "A pla(i)ce for ashes" and not the "Pla(i)ce for everything" quoted in Brunels Tower.

Fig. 41. Fish ashtray 6" (15cm) long. This example is from the Watcombe Pottery.

Fig. 42. Selection of items with a variety of place names from Cockington Forge to Boston, Massachusets and Bermuda. Some of these are miniatures.

Fig. 43 (left). Piping inscription on a dark green ground. Tile for curling tongs lamp by Watcombe.

Fig. 44 (right). Puzzle jug unmarked.

From Mother Earth I claim my Birth,
I'm made a joke for man,
But now I'm here filled with good cheer,
Come taste me if you can.

Longpark

"QUAINT CONCEITS"

PUZZLE jugs are part of a tradition in English pottery that dates back to Mediaeval times. In an article in the *Pottery Gazette* of February 1914 a contributor commented that "there have been many quaint conceits produced in pottery ware . . . and puzzle jugs constitute a by no means small or unimportant phase of freak pottery". Although puzzle jugs have been made since Mediaeval times, their heyday was in the late seventeenth and early eighteenth centuries; these jugs were often ordered by inn or tavern keepers and since it has been estimated that there were over 60,000 of them at that time there was a large potential market. The publican would keep the puzzle jugs for use on suitable convivial occasions when a youth or even a traveller (probably a little the worse for drink) would be invited to drink the contents of the jug without spilling any of the liquor and to thus win a wager. Since this could only be accomplished by sucking from one nozzle whilst carefully arranging the fingers over the other nozzles and holes (a feat which required a clear head!) the wager was usually lost to the amusement of all.

Puzzle jugs varied greatly in form and decoration but the general principle was identical in all. The Torquay puzzle jugs shown in figs. 44 & 45 are examples of the most common form. The jugs had a cylindrical neck which opened out into a bulbous pot; the neck was pierced with holes all the way round thus making it impossible for use in the usual way without spilling any liquor. Around the rim were a number of nozzles which entered a tube encircling the rim and led into the hollow which in turn went into the pot. Torquay puzzle jugs had three nozzles although some of the eighteenth century examples had as many as eight. Liquor (ale or wine) was poured into the globular part of the jug and the novice challenged to taste some of it without spilling any. It was obvious to all but the "blind drunk" that it could not be drunk in the normal way and most guessed that it had to be sucked out through one nozzle. However, the "puzzle" was that there was one inconspicuous hole and unless this was covered it was impossible to drink the ale. This hole was under the top of the handle; thus the experienced "quaffer" could demonstrate how it was possible to suck up the ale whilst it not being apparent to the novice that the "trick" hole was being covered! Obviously this joke could only be played once on each person (although some inns had other versions of the puzzle jug) but in the true tradition of "initiation rites" it could be continued from one generation to the next — and is still being enacted today.

The method of making puzzle jugs was very traditional too because the essential factor was creating a clear tube around the rim and through the handle otherwise the jug would not work. This was done by rolling a thin strip of clay over a piece of string to make the rim and handle — when the pot was fired the string would burn away leaving a tube of uniform thickness.

Torquay puzzle jugs are highly sought after by collectors today; all the major potteries seem to have made them and they have been seen in several sizes and a variety of decorations. The smallest ones were about 3½" tall up to a very large jug 7" tall made by Watcombe; the 4½" version seems to have been the most popular. The scandy was the most common style of decoration; early puzzle jugs (c.1905) usually have scandies either side of the handle and the motto opposite the handle. On later versions of the scandy, and on all other designs the decoration was one side of the handle and the inscription on the reverse like a cup. Exceptions to this were those jugs which had only a motto (see fig. 44). In addition to scandies the cottages and cockerels were also popular decorations but occasionally collectors can find more unusual designs such as the shamrock pattern or butterflies and forget-me-nots (the H1 pattern). One very unusual puzzle jug made by Royal Torquay was decorated with a kingfisher on a blue ground — this was typically coarse and heavily potted but its rarity makes it a desirable additon to a collection.

Fig. 45. A typical Torquay puzzle jug by Longpark 4½" tall (10·6cm).

The mottoes on the Torquay puzzle jugs were most often the two traditional rhymes which have been used for over two centuries and these were:

Here, gentlemen, come try your skill,
I'll hold a wager, if you will,
That you don't drink this liquor all,
But you will spill, or let some fall.

From mother earth I took my birth,
Then form'd a jug by Man,
And now stand here, fill'd with good cheer,
Taste of me if you can.

These two rhymes are believed to have originated in Staffordshire but sometimes another rhyme appeared which probably came from North Devon:

Within this jug there is good liquor,
Tis fit for parson or for vicar,
But how to drink and not to spill,
Will tax the utmost of your skill.

These three mottoes are quite long and required the skills of an accomplished decorator to execute satisfactorily. As the potteries became more competitive and quantity was more important than quality so mottoes became shorter and were often simply maxims such as "If at first you don't succeed, try again".

SEASONS GREETINGS

THE popularity of mottowares which grew during the Edwardian era, was very profitable for the potteries but it also meant that work was increasingly seasonal. During the spring and summer months the potteries were at full stretch trying to meet the demands of the tourist trade. Some of the old potters related how they worked late into the evenings and that their families brought their meals to them to keep the production line going! As they were on piece rates they earned good money. However, in the winter it was a different story. Orders dropped and workers were on short time; often they worked only three days a week and no work meant no money either — except the dole!

One of the ways that the potteries tried to boost sales in these slack periods was by the production of Christmas wares. These pots had either a Christmas decoration or a seasonal motto (occasionally both); some ranges were made for general sale but others were special orders and carry an individual message.

One of the earliest Christmas pieces was a plate made by Aller Vale in 1891 (fig. 46). This was a personalised order for Abbotskerswell Sunday School and has a sgraffito scene of Jesus the Shepherd with a group of children — it is inscribed "Feed my lambs" and has a simple naive charm. John Phillips, the owner of the Aller Vale pottery, was a regular worshipper at Abbotskerswell Church and after his death in 1897 a memorial was erected in the church inscribed "This tablet is erected by the villagers, Sunday School teachers and children of this parish, to commemorate his seventeen years work amongst them". Perhaps the plate was his Christmas gift to the children in 1891.

During the early years of the century the Torquay potteries began to decorate some of their mottowares with holly or mistletoe to give them Christmas appeal. The teapot and tyg shown in fig. 46 by Aller Vale are two examples; these pieces have conventional "multi-purpose" mottoes e.g. "Do not stain todays blue sky with tomorrows clouds" on the tyg. Sometimes seasonal mottoes were used — an example of this is on a jug decorated with holly, also by Aller Vale, which is inscribed:

Old times were good
New times are pleasant
But for wishing you well
No time's like the present.

Watcombe is known to have used a similar holly decoration and occasionally mistletoe on a green ground. Longpark made jugs with a green band of stylised holly.

Many Christmas presents were made by simply incising a personal message on a pot which had a standard decoration. Customers could order these directly from the potteries but sometimes they were gifts from employees to their families. Examples of these are a Royal Torquay biscuit barrel decorated with a yacht in a rosy sunset setting with the message "With best wishes to my wife from George, Xmas 1919". A Watcombe example is a cup and saucer decorated with a scandy pattern and incised "A Happy Xmas to Gertie with love from Doris 1916".

The potteries sometimes received special orders from hotels or other businesses to make "Christmas boxes" that could be given away to their suppliers or customers. Often these were ashtrays or pin trays such as the rectangular tray with a painted greeting "Health and Happiness to you and yours from the Royal Oak Hotel Keswick Xmas 1939"; the decoration on this tray is of geometric shapes painted in yellow, blue and mauve — not at all "Christmassy"!

After World War Two Watcombe introduced a new Christmas line which they called "Winter Cottage Ware" (fig. 46); this was done on a blue ground and the cottage had snow on the roof with a fir (or Christmas) tree, also bedecked in snow, at the side. The mottoes were conventional though, such as "Enough's

Fig. 46. Christmas pieces spanning 70 years. The plate is the earliest having been made at Aller Vale in 1891 for the Abbotskerswell Sunday School. The three handled tyg and the teapot (in the popular 1476 shape) are also Aller Vale c.1915. The jug shows a winter cottage scene on a blue ground; this was made by Watcombe in the 1950s.

as good as a feast" on a plate or "Take a little jam" on a jampot. The Winter Cottage Ware was available in the complete Devon Mottoware range.

Christmas pieces are not easy to find but they are well worth the hunt to add to a collection of mottowares. They can also be used to make a Christmas decoration or, as was originally intended, as a means of saying "Seasons Greetings".

CHRISTMAS

Feed my lambs — Christmas 1891 — Abbotskerswell Sunday School.
Aller Vale

Hope & Anchor Inn — Xmas 1939
Unmarked

DEVON SCENT

PERFUME pots were a major output of virtually all the Torquay potteries from about 1918; indeed the variety of pots is so diverse that they could form a specialist collection in themselves.

The Torquay potteries began to make perfume pots in the 1890s but they were usually part of dressing table sets and were decorated with flowers or scrolls in the style of their art pottery. In the early twentieth century some scent bottles were made in the popular mottowares, for instance, a bottle made by Watcombe decorated with a scandy and inscribed with the motto "Save yourself pains by

Fig. 47. Variations on the scandy pattern. The crudely executed teapot stand at the front is from the short lived Plymouth Gas Fired Pottery c.1926.

taking pains", or a cottage decorated pot inscribed "Blackgang violets". Judging by their scarcity today they were not a popular line. However, soon after the end of World War I a new scent bottle was introduced which was decorated with a violet flower on a cream ground and this became an instant success. It seems likely that Longpark was the first pottery to bring out this line but with its immediate popularity all the other South Devon potteries soon followed suit. Most scent bottles do not have a maker's stamp, but sometimes they can be found marked from Longpark, Watcombe, Royal Torquay, Bovey or Darmouth.

The most popular scent bottles were decorated with a mauve violet on a cream ground but Watcombe also made a version with a white violet on a blue ground. As these were essentially holiday souvenirs they were usually inscribed with suitable mottoes such as "Ye olde Devon violets", "Swanage violets", "Dingley Dell violets" etc. With the success of the violets bottles other scents were made; lavender seems to have been popular but collectors should look for lilac, rose, lilies of the valley, heather, mixed bouquets and even pine. The inscriptions indicate the diversity of the market from Dartmoor heather to Welsh lilac or Skegness Rose. More unusual are those with indeterminate perfumes such as a Royal Torquay bottle decorated with ships inscribed "Blackpool breezes", or a pot decorated with a seagull containing "Clacton breezes"!

Fig. 48. A small variety of the many types of scent bottles.

Scent bottles came in a great variety of shapes, the "squashy" version with dimpled sides probably being the most common. These were made by forming a lump of clay in the hands until it was the right shape and then pushing in one finger to make the scent container — thus the customer only got a fingerful of scent yet they thought they were getting more because the pot was large and heavy! More unusual shapes include a jug with a mauve handle (for the dressing table), a lighthouse, a mushroom with a pixie stopper on top and a tall upright pot which could be used as a candlestick when the scent was used up. Another rare scent container was shaped like a bunch of violets and carried the painted inscription "Ye olde Devon violets, Torquay" (also seen with "Paignton"); on the base is a Registered number: Rgd. 732393. this design was registered in 1927 by Alfred George Cassidy of 22 Fleet Street, Torquay, who carried on the business of Maison Lyons Specialist and then a confectionary — presumably he patented this design for sale in his shop.

Most of the scent bottles were sent by the potteries to perfume manufacturers or dealers for filling: Patemans, Aidees and Bathes were major outlets. The perfume was put into the bottles by pipette and then corked. The tops were then sealed to prevent evaporation; the seal was made with a thin film of plastic which was stored in a special solution to keep it supple. The plastic was put over the cork and tied in place — as it dried out it shrank and became hard thus sealing the pot. The plastic was trimmed to shape and mauve ribbons were tied around the neck. Sometimes a cork with a decorative stopper was also tied round the neck so this could be used instead of the plain cork once the bottle was opened. Many decorative stoppers were made in the form of a crown but the small Devonshire pixies are rarer and sought after by collectors.

In some cases the scent was not placed directly in the pot but instead a small glass phial of scent with a rubber stopper was put in — presumably this was a cheaper method because individual hand filling was very time consuming.

The former employees who worked in the scent bottle trade often had amusing stories to tell about their lives there. One story related to a major chain store which had received complaints that there was no scent in their pots even though the seals were in tact when they were opened. Investigation revealed that a potter had a very long finger nail so that when he made the scent "container" his nail made a small hole right through to the bottom of the pot. The glaze did not fill this crack so the scent gradually seeped out! Other workers vividly remember the strong smell of scent which permeated all their clothes and hair. Some of them also related how many pots got filled with the wrong scent — did the customers ever notice?

Many scent bottles were inscribed with the name of the retailer — "Bathes" and "Boots the Chemists" are probably the most common but others that have been seen include "Bristows", "Evans Chemists Margate", "Stirlings True Irish Violets", "Reeds of Ilfracombe" and a "Souvenir of the Oldest Chymist Shoppe in England, Knaresborough, Yorkshire". The oldest chemist shop did a huge trade in souvenirs made by virtually all the Torquay potteries; items with their inscriptions include jugs, sugar bowls, match strikers, inkwells, egg cups etc.

In the inter-war years Devon violets were really big business as is evident by the stand mounted by Bathes at the South London Exhibition in 1934; a photograph of this "delightful stall" appeared in the *Torquay Times* of 16th March 1934. The whole stand was made to look like a woodland grotto with branches and leaves over the sides and roof; on the stand itself were huge bunches of violets interspersed with scent bottles of all shapes and sizes. Violets perfume pots were sold throughout the United Kingdom and abroad, especially to the British Empire and America. Patemans were shipping to the USA and Canada by 1936 and described their perfume as "Genuine". Bathes called their product "the Original Devon violets perfume" and advertised it as "a glorious perfume reminiscent of the country lanes of dear Old England"; they claimed it was "obtainable from all leading stores throughout the world"! Competition to capture the market was very intense.

In addition to the popular scent bottles, the potteries also made pots decorated with other patterns which form an interesting addition to any collection. Some of these were decorated with a diving kingfisher on a blue ground, or the jazz pattern consisting of geometric splashes of colour. More unusual are those depicting specific places such as Dunster Yarn Market, or a pixie dancing on a mushroom made by Lemon and Crute.

Part of the pleasure in collecting scent bottles is knowing that they are still quite common and relatively cheap! The great diversity of shape, decoration and scent means that it is possible to build up a varied collection fairly easily. Collectors should also look for the rarer items such as pots with a pixie stopper, bottles which still have original paper labels, or for unopened bottles which may still be in their original boxes.

Souvenir from the oldest chymist shoppe in England. Knaresborough, Yorkshire. Est. 1720.

Wishing Well Water — Upwey Wishing Well.

Devon violets — Westward Ho.

Rose of Devon.

Ilfracombe breezes — Reed, Ilfracombe.

Old English lavender — Evans Chemists, Margate.

True Cornish lavender.

Widecombe violets.

Heaven send thee many merry days
Bathes Devon violets — Bath cologne
Torquay, England.

Savernake Forest bouquet
Gautlett, Marlborough.

Various Potteries

HOW MOTTOWARES WERE MADE

"Most tradesmen were on piece-work, and I recall that I had to engrave the mottoes on seven dozen articles an hour to earn one shilling and fourpence."

Len Mayo, potter at the Longpark Pottery 1926–40 (quoted in TPCS newsletter January 1978).

1. First of all the clay had to be cleaned and mixed to the correct consistency; it was then formed into balls of the right weight for the article to be made. The pots were made in several different ways:

(a) Vases, Teapots, Jugs, etc. were formed on the wheel by throwers; they would then be left to dry to a leather state ready for smoothing by turners.

(b) Plates were formed by pushing the

Fig. 49. Plate decorated with heather on a blue ground and piped inscription. Longpark c.1930. 10¾in (27·4cm) diameter.

clay on to a former and shaping it to a uniform thickness using a jigger.

(c) Cups were made by pushing the clay into a mould and shaping it with a jolley.

(d) Items such as grotesque Cats were made by pushing clay into moulds. When the clay had hardened the sections were joined together using slip.

2. When the pots were leather hard and smoothed they were taken to the slip dipping shop to be coated in a thin film of slip. Slip was a creamy mixture of white clay and water; sometimes dyes were added to produce green or blue or other shades of slips for covering white clay items. The pots were dipped in the bucket of slip, excess wiped away and left to dry.

3. When the slip base had hardened the decoration was applied, either by painting with coloured slips or with pigment. Then the motto was either scratched through the base using a long nail or painted on with pigments.

Fig. 50. Fred Dart at the potters wheel at Aller Vale throwing a cylinder vase c.1920.

I watched the Potter thumping his wet clay,
And with its all obliterated tongue it murmured,
Gently Brother! Gently pray.
Watcombe

Fig. 51. John Dart dipping a "1476" shaped teapot into the slip bucket at Aller Vale c.1900.

4. The pots were now ready for their first firing in the biscuit oven having been carefully packed into saggars; these are clay boxes which fit into the kiln.

5. After firing and cooling, a process which took several days, the pots were then ready for glazing. Glazes were kept in buckets and the items dipped in them.

6. Once the glaze had hardened off the pots were again packed into saggars and were fired in the glost kiln.

7. The mottowares were now ready for dispatching to customers all over the world.

Fig. 52 (above): Watcombe Pottery c.1919. Middle, Charlie Wonnacott; right, Ernie Clements?; on left Arthur Cole? Fig. 53 (below): The Longpark Pottery Company c.1920.

THE "1476" TEASET

THE 1476 shape was undoubtedly the most widely used shape of all in the South Devon potteries — items made in this shape were teapots, sugar basins and milk jugs as in the photograph (fig. 54). The shape was first introduced around the turn of the century; a scandy teapot was illustrated in the *Pottery Gazette* in 1903 in an advertisement for the Royal Aller Vale and Watcombe Art Pottery. Watcombe were still making 1476 teasets in 1962, the year the pottery closed. The shape probably originated at the Aller Vale pottery but it was adopted at Watcombe when the companies came under common ownership in 1901 and other potteries copied the shape too, especially Longpark, Royal Torquay and Barton.

A seemingly endless variety of patterns were used to decorate 1476 teasets. Cottages are the most common but all the popular mottoware patterns were used. Other patterns that have been seen include shamrocks, thistles, the Widecombe Fair characters, seagulls on a blue ground, and multi-coloured scrolls on a cream ground (the B1 pattern) with the inscription "From Niagara Falls, Canada". In addition, many art pottery decorations have been seen ranging from the "Dutch style" windmills to "Green Art Wares" and Alexandra roses or geometric Art Deco designs; these are outside the scope of this book though.

The 1476 teapots were made in a wide variety of sizes too. The smallest ones held just 5 fluid ounces and were part of a dolls teaset; the largest were giant teapots (see front cover) which held 8½ pints, or 40 cups, and were made for teashops. In between these there were several other sizes but four became standard lines: ½ pint, 1 pint, 1½ pints and 2 pints.

It is fascinating to look at old advertisements and catalogues to see the prices of Torquay pottery when it was originally sold. Because the 1476 shape was so enduring it provides a useful reference to compare changing fashions in decoration as well as a price guide.

Fig. 54. The 1476 teaset Watcombe . . .

Jarrold and Sons Ltd., a department store in Norwich, advertised a selection of Torquay pottery in their catalogues of c.1912; included were Aller Vale 1476 scandy teapots in three sizes at 1/- (5 pence), 1/4½ and 2/- each — unfortunately the catalogue did not give the capacities of the teapots. Sugar bowls and cream jugs, one size only, were priced at 1/- the pair. The prices in the Jarrold catalogue were the retail prices and obviously give no indication of wholesale prices from the pottery.

A Longpark catalogue of the 1930s listed a wide range of 1476 teapots. The patterns on offer were: scandy (called "conventional decoration"), black cockerel, coloured cockerel, thistle, shamrock and ship; perhaps surprisingly, there were no cottage decorations in the catalogue. There were four sizes of teapot available in all the listed patterns: small size, ½ pint, at 10/- (50 pence) a dozen; medium size, 1 pint, at 16/- dozen; large size, 1½ pints, at 20/- dozen, and extra large, 2 pints, at 27/- dozen. Sugars and cream jugs came in three sizes and were sold separately at 4/6, 7/- and 9/- dozen. Customers could have the name of a town added for an additional charge of 5%; however, for orders over £5 no extra charge was made.

By the 1950s inflation had caused the price of mottowares to escalate as can be seen from a Watcombe price list of 1958. Small size 1476 teapots were now 57/- (£2.85) a dozen, medium size 73/- dozen, large size 91/- dozen and extra large size 136/- dozen. Watcombe made two sizes of sugar bowl and cream jug and these were sold in pairs at 36/6 and 46/3 a dozen. Watcombe were offering only three decorations in the 1476 range: cottages, winter cottages and ships, and the only other mottoware decoration shown in the catalogue was the Lucky Devon Pixie which was made in a very limited range. Designs such as shamrocks and thistles had been continued by Watcombe after World War Two but by the late 1950s when the popularity of mottowares went into sharp decline, the styles were severely curtailed.

Collectors sometimes like to make up teasets of teapot, sugar bowl, cream or milk jug and perhaps cups and saucers and plates. Care must be taken to ensure that the items really are sets and not mis-matches. A 1476 set comprises the items as shown in the photograph: the teapot, jug and bowl should all be the flat angular shape and the style of decoration and borders should also match. The correct cups should be straight sided, slightly tapering in towards the base. Sometimes dealers offer "sets" that are mis-matches and insist they are correct because "I bought them like that from a house sale"! This may well be true, but it is important to remember that mottoware teasets were originally bought for use and inevitably items would get broken — they would often be replaced by similar items which would not necessarily match. In some cases teasets have been seen made up of pieces with the same decoration e.g. scandy, but with shapes that do not match and items from different potteries! Complete teasets including cups and saucers and plates, for six people are very rarely found and making up a set can prove a difficult task given the huge variations in mottowares.

Jist a wee drappie tea
Aller Vale

Up to the lips and over the gums,
Look out tummy here it comes.
Watcombe

T.P.C.S. MOTTOES

A Cornish Litany.
From Ghoulies and Ghosties and Long Leggity Beasties,
And things that go bump in the night,
Good Lord deliver us.

A wet sheet, a flowing sail,
And a mind thats blowing free. (AV)

A safe conscience makes a sound sleep. (W)

A car on the road is worth two in the ditch. (UM late)

As I was going to St. Ives,
I met a man with seven wives,
Each wife had seven sacks,
Each sack had seven cats,
Each cat had seven kits,
Kits, cats, sacks and wives,
How many were going to St. Ives?
(Answer: One, on reverse) (W)

A woman's face may be a Chemist's fortune. (W)

A pound of pluck is worth a load of luck. (L)

A still tongue makes a wise head. (TP)

A safe conscience makes a sound sleep. (AV)

A little explained, a little endured,
A little forgiven, and the quarrel is cured. (AV)

Be always as merry as ever you can
For few will delight in a sorrowful man. (HME)

Be strong, Be good, Be pure,
The Right only shall endure. (L)

Be like the sundial, Count only the sunny hours. (Dartmouth)

Brevity is the soul of wit.
(Shakespeare) (W)

Contrivance is better than force. (W)

Cyder doth stir up the mind,
And awakens a desire to eat. (W)

Don't cry over spilt milk
There's water in it already. (W)

Do what you can, being what you are,
Shine like a glowworm, if you can't be a star. (AV)

Don't grouse,
Work like Helen B. Merry. (W)

Don't give your husband too much rope,
He might skip. (W)

Drink puppy drink. (W)

Early to bed, early to rise,
Makes a man healthy, wealthy and wise. (AV)

First deserve then desire. (AV)

From Mother Earth I claim my Birth,
I'm made a joke for man,
But now I'm here filled with good cheer,
Come taste me if you can. (L)

Good courage breaks ill luck. (L)

Here's to beefsteak when you're hungry,
Beer when you're dry,
fivers when you're hard up,
Heaven when you die. (W)

He that buys land buys many stones,
He that buys flesh buys many bones,
He that buys eggs buys many shells,
He that buys ale buys nothing else. (W)

Have not your cloak to make,
When it begins to rain. (W)

Haste trips up its own heels. (L)

He may do what he will,
That will do what he can. (L)

He that must thrive,
Must rise at five. (HME)

Home the spot on earth supremely blest. (HME)

Hold me tight and don't be clumsy,
Or you'll break this mug from Romsey. (W)

Hope for the best, look for the best,
The worst will never appear,
Pray for the best then leave the rest,
God always answers a prayer. (L)

Good examples are best sermons. (W)

How to make a profit following horses.
From Grandpa 3274 Bedford. (W)
(Personalised ashtray for a Bookmaker.)

I watched the Potter thumping his wet clay,
And with its all obliterated tongue it murmured,
Gently Brother! Gently pray. (W)

I always have a drink at eleven,
Its a duty that has to be done,
If I can't have one at eleven,
I have eleven at one. (W)

Improve time in time while time lasts,
For all time is no time when time is past. (AV)

Influence is jolly useful,
Until you've used it.

I wish you all the joy that you may wish. (HME)

If you can't climb — fly. (L)

If you can't lift the stone,
Perhaps you can roll it. (L)

If you've got to do something for nothing,
Do it for yourself. (L)

If water rots your boots,
What the hell does it do to your stomach. (W)

Its better to wear out than rust out. (W)

Dawntee laive a stone in the road,
Vur zumbody else to val over'n. (AV)

If you're not a beauty,
Be happy that you're plain,
Be a wheel greaser,
If you can't drive a train. (W)

Junket is the dish of Devon,
A better dish is hard to find,
This is everyone's opinion,
Excepting those who're out of mind. (L)

Its a comely fashion to be glad,
Joy is the grace we say to God. (L)

Love your enemies, trust but few,
And always paddle your own canoe. (L)

Life were not worth the living,
If no one were the better,
For having met you on the way,
And known the sunshine of your stay. (AV)

Life is a struggle not a race,
A wise man keeps an even pace. (AV)

Life is mostly froth and bubble,
Two things stand as stone,
Kindness in another's trouble,
Courage in your own. (L)

Life is an echo, it all comes back,
The good, the false, the true,
So give from your heart, the best you can,
And the best will return to you. (L)

Many a (batchelor) ship has been wrecked
On a permanent wave. (W)

Many a sorrow we forget,
Through pipe, cigar or cigarette. (W)

Men make houses, women make homes. (HME)

May you never find a mouse in your cupboard,
With tears in its eyes. (L)

My fairest child, I have no song to give you,
No lark could pipe to skies as dull and grey,
Yet ere we part, one lesson I can leave you,
For every day, Be good sweet maid and let who will be clever,
Do noble things, not dream them all day long,
And so make life, death and that vast forever,
One grand sweet song! (L)

Man's inhumanity to man makes countless thousands mourn. (AV)

Night brings out stars as sorrow shows us truths. (W)

O're the green and balmy meadow,
Where the milky kine repose. (HME)

No life can be dreary, when work is delight. (UM)

Rosey Posey at five takes Tea,
Dolls and kittens invited free. (L)

Strength for Today is all that we need,
For there never will be a Tomorrow,
Tomorrow is but another Today,
With its own measure of joy and sorrow. (W)

Sandy love the Thistle,
John Bull loves the Rose,
But Paddy loves the land,
Where the shamrock grows. (AV)

Soft words win hard hearts. (W)

Some like apples,
Some like inions,
So many men,
So many 'pinions. (AV)

Read	see	that	me	but	not	my	got
down	will	I	love	if	me	love	for
and	you	love	you	that	love	for	be
up	and	you	if	you	should	you	must

(AV)

Save and spend and God will send.
(HME)

The red kine bathing in the stream
just below the clammer,
The music of the bird and bee,
The scythe and blacksmith's hammer.
Dear old Devon. (AV)

There's no time like now.
(Royal Torquay)

The island in winter is slack as can be
Sometimes its worse than the far west
countree,
But once in the season — the strain on
poor Ted,
Is terrific! Its hell! He can't get to bed.
(W)

Think not of tomorrow's child of the King,
Leave them in His hand do the next best
thing. (AV)

They can who think they can,
Adventures are to the adventurous. (AV)

Take thy calling thankfully,
Love thy neighbour neighbourly,
Shun the path to beggary. (UM)

Too much sit down break trousers. (UM)

The mill will never grind with the water
that is past. (AV)

To teach his grandson draughts,
His leisure he'd employ,
Until at last the old man,
Was beaten by the boy. (L)

This is a world to live in
To buy, spend, or to give in,
But to beg, borrow, or get a man's own,
Such a world was never known. (L)

The tempest that disturbs the water,
Reveals the Rock. (W)

Uneasy lies the head that tells a good
many of them. (UM)

Up to the lips and over the gums,
Look out tummy here it comes. (W)

Vessels large may venture more
Little boats must keep the shore. (AV)

Work on, Hope on, Self help is noble
schooling,
You do you best and leave the rest,
To God's Almighty ruling. (AV)

When in the pink, Write with this ink.
(L)

Wishes never filled the bag. (L)

We must be kind but not in words alone.
(L)

When the great scorer comes
To write against your name
He writes not if you won or lost
But how you played the game. (L)

We must take the current as it serves
Or lose our venture. (W)

Wishee well and wishee honest. (UM)

Whichever way the wind doth blow
Someone is glad to have it so.

When your head feels queer
And your breath smells strong,
And you laugh like hell at any old song,
You're drunk old man, you're drunk. (W)

Be just and fear not
(Henry VIII Act V) (HM)

To be or not to be, that is the question
(Hamlet Act III) (HM)

Honor and shame from no conditions rise
Act well your part, there all the honor lies
(Shakespeare) (HM)

In sweet music is such art
Killing care and grief of heart (HM)

Them that winna work maun want.

We thank thee Lord vur this gude bankit,
Which us a had tugether,
An' give us Grace tu work apace,
That us may airn another. (W)

Temps pommele, fille fardee
Ne sont pas de longue duree
Time dappled cloudy weather
Painted girl
They are not of long duration (HM)

He that by the plough would thrive
Himself must either holde or drive
(AV)

The lucky have their days and those they chose
The unlucky have their hours and those they lose (AV)

Small herbs have grace
Ill weeds grow apace (AV)

Half the worlds mischief, folly and woe
Comes from a 'Yes' that ought to be 'No'
(L)

For heather bells and wild bee roves
A' natures creatures hae their loves
(HM)

Come my old friends and take a pot
But mark now what I say
When thou drinkest thy neighbours health
Drink not thine own away
1822 (HME)

One good friend is worth many relations
(L)

Thur now, du'ee you'en?
Daunt like Craim
Way, yu niver had noan.

God hath often a great share in a little home (W)

Teddy Bears' Picnic. (RW)

The evil that men do lives after them.
(Shakespeare, *Julius Caesar*) (AV)

Dawnt'ee buden todays strength
With tomorrows clouds. (L)

Fair be all the hopes and prosperous be thy life in peace or war. (HM)

Don't be a crank
Be a self starter. (W)

He who gave thee this ring of gold
Tis he who shall cherish when thou art old.
(W)

A hungry man's an angry man. (UM)

Guid will neer want true tae show itsel.
(AV)

What is the difference between
1st A Rich Scotsman
2nd A Poor Scotsman
3rd A Dead Scotsman P.T.O.

On the reverse of the ashtray is the answer.

1st Has a canopy over his bed.
2nd Has a canopy under his bed.
3rd Canna P at all. (W)

YY UR YY UB
YY UR the 1 for me. (UM)

SCOTLAND

A thing has an end, and a pudding has twa (L)

Jist a wee drappie tea (AV)

Stracht frae the hen (AV)

Dinna scrimp the craim (AV)

Hang hunger and droon drouth. (W)

Help yersel an dinna be blate,
Parritch makes the man. (L)

Stracht frae the Coo (AV)

Deal sma' an' serve a' (L)

Ilka dog has his day. (L)

Better wear shoon than sheets. (L)

Tak yer wull o't. (L)

Ca' yer ain girr ne'er heed yer neebors.
(AV)

Fig. 55. Plate, 11in (28cm) diameter made by Longpark. This crocus pattern was very popular in the 1930s.

A guid tale can be twice tauld. (L)

There's as guid fish in the sea
As ever cam' oot o' it. (L)

Dinna be aye ettlin
But juist write at aince. (AV)

Noo is the day and noo is the hour. (HME)

Ower reckless may repent. (HME)

A word frae ye's neist tae a word wi'ye. (AV)

For a' that and a' that
It's coming yet, for a' that,
That man to man the world o'er,
Shall brothers be for a' that. (W)

The de'ils aye kin' tae his ain. (L)

A reeky house and a guirnin wife,
Will lead a man a fashious life. (L)

WELSH
Deuparth rhodd yw ewyllys.
A will is a twice given gift. (AV)

Gwell angnan na chy wily dd
Better sorrow than shame. (HME)

O geiniog i geiniog
Ar arian yn bunt.
Penny to penny makes a pound. (L)

Bwythyn Cymreig (Welsh Cottage) (W)

Oni heuir ni fedir.
If you don't sew you will not reap. (AV)

ISLE OF MAN (MANX)
Kys ta shin.
Time enough. (W)

ADVERTISING
Wishing Well Water — Labrador Bay (nr. Torquay) (W)

Wishing Well Water — Upwey Wishing Well. (W)

Souvenir from the oldest chymist shoppe in England.
Knaresborough, Yorkshire. Est 1720. (W)

Freyland Ale — Whenever I drink of Freyland Ale
Drawn from an old brown bottle,
I feel as if a summer morn
Was running down my throttle —
(Ammon Wrigley)
(R.Torquay)

PERSONAL
Marjoria Garvey — May 14th 1917 (L)

CANADA
Muskoka — Many are called but few get up.

MOARI — NEW ZEALAND
Marama Nui A Magi Kei Riro i A Noho.
Your work has brought much light at the time of my departure. (L)

Meatia Atu He Mea Mau.
A present to you from abroad. (L)

Meatie Atu He Kirimi Mau.
A present for you for Christmas. (L)

CHRISTMAS
Feed my lambs — Christmas 1891 — Abbotskerswell Sunday School. (AV)

Hope & Anchor Inn — Xmas 1939 (UM)

MUSIC HALL CATCHPHRASE
Its turned out nice again — George.
(George Formby — comedian) (W)

THE LORD'S PRAYER
Our Father, which art in heaven,
Hallowed be thy Name,
Thy Kingdom come,
Thy will be done,
In earth as it is in heaven.
Give us this day our daily bread
And forgive us our trespasses,
As we forgive them that trespass against us.
And lead us not into temptation,
But deliver us from evil.
For thine is the Kingdom,
The power and the glory,
For ever and ever. Amen. (L)